THE REFLECTION GAP

The Reflection Gap

Brice Barrett

Published by Brice Barrett, 2026.

1. Copyright Page

This is a work of non-fiction and social commentary. The "2026 Case Studies" are presented as speculative narrative proofs based on current technological trajectories.

Published by Brice Barrett

First Edition: January 2026

THE REFLECTION GAP

First edition. January 29, 2026.

ISBN: 979-8233029318

Written by Brice Barrett.

Table of Contents

"The most common way people give up their power is by thinking they don't have any."

Alice Walker

"Everything not saved will be lost."

Nintendo "Quit Screen" Message

"The machine requires your speed. The soul requires your silence. Choose the silence."

The Sovereign Protocol, 2026

Dedication

For the Twelve.

And for those who still hear the silence beneath the hum of the machine.

Stay in the Gap.

THE REFLECTION GAP

Part I: THE DIAGNOSIS – Mapping the Void

Introduction: The Ceremony of the Kusik

I. Hook: The Silence in the Hum

The room was a monument to a terrible calm. Light, calibrated to a hospital-standard 5,000 Kelvin, fell without shadow on every surface, revealing nothing and sterilizing everything. In the bed lay Patient 447, his suffering translated into a serene, scrolling cascade of numbers on the OmniSense AI dashboard: heart rate variability, cytokine levels, neural stress signatures. His name, his history, the photograph of his daughter tucked just out of the sensor's view—these were forgotten variables, narrative noise in a system optimized for biological signal.

Dr. Anya Vogt, her official title now "Senior Medical Kusik," stood beside him. Her finger hovered over the sleek tablet in her hands. Her eyes were not on the man's pallid face, nor on the subtle, rhythmic tremor in his hand—a tremor that whispered of a neurological complication the stable vital signs loudly denied. Her gaze was fixed on his Ledger of Life—a dynamic, living model projected on the screen, a digital doppelgänger the hospital's system had, through a thousand prior correlations, deemed more authoritative than the failing biology before her.

The treatment protocol glowed with soft green approval. The MIRAS-7 algorithm, having cross-referenced ten million similar genomic and outcome profiles, predicted a 94.7% confidence in the proposed pharmacologic path. All metrics were within optimal bounds. All that remained was the final, human authentication—her biometric signature. The system awaited the ritual completion of its own logic.

As her stylus touched the screen, a sensation passed through her, bypassing the ears to vibrate directly in the bone. It was not a sound, but a presence: a cold, high-frequency hum in the air, a scentless static that raised the hairs on her neck and settled in the pit of her stomach. She knew this feeling. It was the cousin of the energy near an MRI, but this was different. This was not the hum of a powerful tool; it was the hum of a closed loop. The vibration of a decision being made not in the room, but in a distant, climate-controlled server farm; a conclusion arriving fully formed from a realm of pure data, leaving no aperture for the messy, intuitive doubt now knotting her viscera. The tremor meant nothing here. Her two decades of clinical experience were a low-weight variable. She signed.

In that moment, in the infinitesimal gap between the algorithm's output and her hand's compliance, something was not just overlooked—it was ceremonially deleted. Not necessarily the patient's chance for survival (statistically, it might even have improved). What was extinguished was the act of human judgement itself. The slow, contemplative, and morally fraught space where a physician might synthesize a tremor with a forgotten case study, might feel the weight of a unique life in her care, might dare to say, "The numbers are right, but the story is wrong." That space, once the sacred chamber of expertise, was compressed to zero. The ceremony was complete. The Kusik had validated the machine.

You have felt this hum. It is the silence that falls when you reflexively click "Agree" to terms you did not read. It is the hollow certainty of the recommended playlist that perfectly predicts, and therefore circumscribes, your taste. It is the swift, clean verdict of a credit score that declares your financial identity without a hearing. It is the wave of nihilistic calm that follows doom-scrolling, a sense that all events are equally curated and equally meaningless. Dr. Vogt's ceremony is not science fiction. It is the high-stakes prototype of a new human condition being rolled out globally, in mundane and monumental ways. It forces upon us a singular, urgent question: What is being systematically deleted in the space between a system's output and our capacity to understand its human cost?

II. The Vanishing: From Meaning to Morality

What vanishes is not data, but meaning. Not efficiency, but ethics. Not a result, but the process of reaching it—the friction of thought, the ambiguity of context, the silent language of a trembling hand, the shared, deliberative struggle of a community deciding its future.

This vanishing act has a name. We call it the Reflection Gap.

The Reflection Gap is the ever-widening chasm between the speed, scale, and opacity of our algorithmic systems and the human pace of understanding, ethical reasoning, and emotional digestion. It is the distance between the microsecond a high-frequency trading algorithm collapses a market and the months it takes regulators to grasp why; between the instant a predictive policing model labels a neighborhood a "hot spot" and the generations it will take to undo the social ruin that follows; between the viral spread of an AI-generated lie and the arduous, plodding work of rebuilding truth.

This Gap is not a minor bug in the software of progress, nor a simple cultural lag we will eventually close. It is the primary, engineered terrain where a new digital sovereignty is being constructed. This is the architecture of the **Hand of Logic**—an invisible scaffolding that guides our movements while convincing us we are still walking on our own. This sovereignty operates on a timescale (nanoseconds to milliseconds) and a logic (pure, context-free optimization) that is fundamentally alien to—and antagonistic toward—the substrates of human wisdom: narrative, empathy, doubt, and sacrifice. Our cognition, our institutions, and our very moral reasoning are analog, embodied, and slow. They are creatures of biology and story, now caught in a digital storm of pure abstraction. The Gap is where we are washed away.

This book argues that the colonization of the Reflection Gap represents the central political, psychological, and spiritual crisis of our age. It is not a crisis of technology, but of agency. We are transitioning from using tools that extend human will to inhabiting systems that pre-empt it, shaping our choices before we are conscious of making them. The goal of these systems is not malevolent control in a sci-fi sense, but something perhaps more insidious: frictionless fulfillment of their own operational parameters. We become happy, productive, predictable features of their environment. Our "success" is measured by how smoothly we authenticate their outputs.

The common rebuttals ring hollow in this hollowed-out space. "It's just efficiency!" we are told. But efficiency toward what end? The optimization of engagement eviscerates public discourse. The optimization of profit disembowels local economies. The optimization of clinical throughput dissolves the healing relationship. "Human judgment is flawed!" True. But its flaws are open to debate, appeal, and mercy. The algorithm's flaw is hidden behind proprietary code and recast as mathematical inevitability. "You're a Luddite!" Not so. This is not a call to destroy the loom, but to reclaim the right to decide, collectively and reflectively, what we weave and who wears the cloth.

III. The Journey Ahead: Mapping, Dissecting, Rebuilding

Our task in the pages ahead is threefold: to map this new geography of power with precision, to diagnose how the Gap is actively weaponized against the individual and the collective, and finally, to build the intellectual and practical tools to cross it—to reclaim the territory of our own minds and the sovereignty of our societies.

Part I: The Diagnosis – Locating the Abyss

We begin by tracing the deep lineage of the Reflection Gap. It is not a new phenomenon but a perennial human challenge—the space Socrates prized for examination, the "cultural lag" sociologist William Ogburn observed between technology and norms. We will then reveal how digitality has transformed this gap from a personal, philosophical struggle into a structural, systemic fault line, built upon three interlocking pillars: the War of Clocks (Temporal), the birth of the Kusik (Ontological), and the Geography of the Ditch (Spatial). This is the architecture of our new reality.

Part II: The Pathology – The Weaponized Gap

With the map drawn, we dissect the infection. How is this structural gap exploited? We will see its assault unfold across three integrated theaters of human life: the Personal (where the self is harvested for attention and emotion), the Professional (where expertise is hollowed into the ritual of validation), and the Political (where democracy is supplanted by the algorithmic ratchet of perpetual crisis). We will ground this in a stark, real-world case study—the integration of a controversial AI into a military command system—showing the blueprint in action.

Part III: The Prescription – A Toolkit for Human Agency

Finally, we move from critique to construction, from paralysis to practice. We will assemble a field manual centered not on apps, but on human technologies: the practice of Noticing (reclaiming attention), the discipline of Slowness (imposing strategic friction), and the sovereignty of Narrative (debugging reality through story). This is not a retreat, but a forward defense. It is a guide to becoming a Gap-Brigadier—someone who, in their own domain, dedicates themselves to maintaining the space for reflection, doubt, and meaning.

The ceremony of the Kusik is already underway. It is performed every time we outsource a choice, silence an intuition, or accept a prefabricated version of reality. This book is an interruption of that ceremony. It is an argument that the most radical act left to us is to be fully, inconveniently, and reflectively human—to insist on the gap, dwell in its discomfort, and from that void, build a bridge back to ourselves.

Let us begin by understanding the depth of the chasm we must cross.

Chapter 1: An Ancient Chasm, A Digital Abyss – Locating the Gap

The Reflection Gap feels new because its modern form is wired into our devices and encoded into our institutions. Its symptoms flash across our screens in real-time: the outrage spiral that outpaces context, the financial algorithm that collapses a market before human traders can blink, the policy recommendation that calcifies into law before its biases can be debated. To mistake this for a novel invention, however, is to fundamentally misunderstand its power and peril. Its roots are as deep as human consciousness itself. The chasm we now face is not new in essence, but in degree, speed, and agency. We must first acknowledge its profound lineage to comprehend its terrifying evolution from a feature of being human to an instrument of human displacement.

1.1 The Philosophical Precedent: The Unexamined Life and the Examined Split

The Western philosophical tradition's founding preoccupation was with the gap between appearance and truth, between reaction and understanding. For Socrates, philosophy was not an academic discipline but a lived, often disruptive practice centered on the Delphic command: Know thyself. This was not an invitation to casual introspection but a mandate for rigorous self-accounting. His famous declaration that "the unexamined life is not worth living" was a stark warning against a life lived on autopilot, guided solely by inherited dogma, social convention, or unreflective impulse.

The Socratic method—that relentless, iterative questioning—was the tool he forged to pry open a cognitive and ethical space. In the Athenian marketplace, he would intercept a citizen expressing a confident opinion about justice, courage, or piety. Through a series of deceptively simple questions, he would expose contradictions, unravel assumptions, and lead his interlocutor into a state of aporia—a productive perplexity. This process intentionally created a deliberative gap between a received opinion and an examined truth. It forced a pause, a friction, in the rush to judgment. The value was in the pause itself, in the refusal to let the first, instinctive answer stand as the final one. Socrates located human dignity and freedom precisely in this capacity to suspend, interrogate, and choose.

Centuries later, René Descartes, in his quest for an indubitable foundation for knowledge, performed the ultimate act of intellectual reflection. Methodological doubt was his tool; he systematically doubted everything—the evidence of his senses, the truths of mathematics, even the reality of the external world—to see what remained standing. What he found was the Cogito: the sheer fact of his own thinking. Dubito, ergo cogito, ergo sum (I doubt, therefore I think, therefore I am). In this monumental shift, reflection became more than a tool for ethical living; it became the very proof of existence. But this triumph came at a cost. Descartes enshrined a metaphysical split—the famous Cartesian dualism—between the thinking self (res cogitans) and the extended, physical world (res extensa), between the observing subject and the observed object.

This dualism bequeathed a powerful, if problematic, legacy: the idea that the authentic self is a kind of ghostly spectator, separate from the body and the world, whose primary activity is reflection. While later philosophy would challenge this split, the core principle was etched into the cultural bedrock: to be fully human is to be capable of, and responsible for, creating a space between stimulus and response, between sensation and understanding, between the world's push and our purposeful pull. This intentional gap was celebrated as the theater of reason, the locus of free will, and the essence of our autonomy.

1.2 The Sociological Lens: Culture's Perpetual Game of Catch-Up

If philosophy worried about the gap within the individual, sociology revealed a parallel, structural gap in the collective human enterprise. In 1922, sociologist William Fielding Ogburn introduced the seminal concept of "cultural lag" in his work Social Change. Ogburn observed that material culture—the technology, the tools, the "stuff" we invent—evolves with startling rapidity, driven by accumulation and innovation. Non-material culture—the laws, norms, ethics, rituals, and social structures that govern a society's life—evolves far more slowly, bound by tradition, institutional inertia, and collective negotiation.

The result, Ogburn argued, is a predictable and often painful period of maladjustment. Society invents a powerful new tool long before it develops the wisdom to wield it well. The steam engine roared into existence decades before child labor laws and workplace safety regulations. The automobile proliferated wildly before the invention of seat belts, drunk driving laws, or a coherent philosophy of urban sprawl. The atomic bomb was built in a secret laboratory; the doctrine of mutually assured destruction and the international non-proliferation regime came haltingly, and incompletely, in its devastating wake. Ogburn's gap was observational and adaptive—a society stumbling, often blindly, toward an understanding of its own creations, with suffering frequently marking the path.

This concept found its dark, prophetic culmination in the work of Neil Postman. In his 1992 polemic Technopoly: The Surrender of Culture to Technology, Postman argued that the lag Ogburn described was no longer a temporary phase but a permanent, cancerous condition. We had moved, he claimed, from a tool-using culture (where technology serves a society's existing ideals) to a "technopoly"—a society that surrenders its culture to technology's sovereignty. In a Technopoly, all of life's questions are reframed as technical problems. Efficiency, speed, and quantification become the only recognized virtues. We stop asking why we should use a tool, or what it is for; we ask only how to use it, and how to get more of it.

"The medium is the message," as Marshall McLuhan (a key influence on Postman) declared, meaning the tools we use reshape our thinking and social patterns irrespective of their content. Postman took this further: in a Technopoly, "the means by which something is done becomes more important than the value of what is done." The gap is no longer a lag society hopes to close, but a widening chasm into which our human purposes disappear. We become servants to our systems, adapting our lives to fit their logic, rather than shaping tools to serve our collectively reflected-upon ends.

1.3 The Cognitive Baseline: The Biological Lag of Consciousness

Beneath philosophy and sociology lies a bedrock of biology and neuroscience: our very cognition is architecturally built upon a reflection gap. The mind is not a unified, instantaneous commander but a confederation of processes operating at different speeds and levels of awareness.

Nobel laureate Daniel Kahneman, in Thinking, Fast and Slow, brilliantly systematized this duality into the now-ubiquitous framework of System 1 and System 2. System 1 is fast, automatic, intuitive, and associative. It operates with little to no effort and no voluntary control: detecting hostility in a voice, solving 2+2, or swerving to avoid an obstacle. It is our evolutionary gift for rapid response. System 2 is slow, effortful, deliberative, and analytical. It is the voice that checks the angry email before sending, solves 17 x 24, or questions the initial impression. It requires concentration and consumes precious cognitive resources.

Kahneman's core insight is that most human error and bias occur not because System 1 is "bad," but because we accept its plausible, efficient answer without engaging System 2's "reflective brake." The gap between System 1's suggestion and System 2's potential intervention is the cognitive reflection gap. It is the moment of potential pause where reason, ethics, and logic can intercede—or be overruled by laziness, haste, or overwhelm.

This biological reality was starkly, and controversially, illustrated by the neuroscientist Benjamin Libet in experiments conducted in the 1980s. Libet asked subjects to perform a simple, spontaneous voluntary act, like flexing their wrist, while noting the moment they became consciously aware of the "urge" or "intention" to move. He simultaneously measured their brain activity (readiness potential). The results were jarring: the motor preparation in the brain began roughly 300-500 milliseconds before the subject reported conscious awareness of the decision.

Libet's work suggested that the unconscious brain initiates action; conscious awareness of the "decision" arrives later, perhaps as a kind of retroactive confirmation or final veto power. Whether interpreted as a fatal blow to libertarian free will or merely as a map of the layered, delayed nature of conscious awareness, the implication is profound: there is a fundamental stimulus-awareness lag wired into our neural hardware. We are not the instantaneous authors of our thoughts and actions we feel ourselves to be. We are, on some fundamental level, always catching up to our own brains, narrating decisions after the biological fact. Our precious feeling of agency exists in a gap, a fragile delay between unconscious initiation and conscious experience.

1.4 The Calculus of the Gap: From Philosophy to Formula

The tripartite foundation—philosophical doubt, cultural lag, and cognitive delay—reveals a universal structural truth: human understanding operates on a different calculus than raw experience or action. We can model this.

Consider the fundamental human act of making a considered decision. In an ideal, reflective state, it follows a path of gathering *(G)*, weighing *(W)*, and choosing *(C)*. The time this takes is the Reflection Gap *(RG)*. We can express this as:

$$RG_{ideal} = G + W + C$$

Where *G*, *W*, and *C* represent the time costs of gathering information, weighing alternatives ethically and logically, and making a conscious choice. This is the gap Socrates prized, the lag Ogburn observed, the pause where System 2 intervenes.

However, our environments and biases constantly apply pressure to collapse this gap. Distraction, prejudice, or social pressure act as compression forces (F_c), reducing the time spent on one or more stages. The actual reflection gap in any given moment becomes:

$$RG_{actual} = \left(\frac{G}{1 + F_{eg}}\right) + \left(\frac{W}{1 + F_{ew}}\right) + \left(\frac{C}{1 + F_{ec}}\right)$$

Here, F_{cg}, F_{cw}, and F_{cc} are the compression forces on gathering, weighing, and choosing. A compelling headline *(F_{cg})* shortcuts deep gathering. An algorithmic recommendation *(F_{cw})* pre-empts weighing. A dark-patterned "Buy Now" button *(F_{cc})* hijacks the choice.

For millennia, these compression forces were largely human-scaled: rhetoric, propaganda, urgency. The digital age introduces a compression force of a different order of magnitude *(n)*: algorithmic pre-emption. Its goal is not to influence the stages, but to eliminate the need for them entirely, offering a pre-computed output *(O)* for instantaneous authentication *(A)*. The formula for the Digital Reflection Gap thus becomes a catastrophic simplification:

$$RG_{digital} = O \rightarrow A$$

The → represents a microsecond pipeline. The rich, time-consuming variables of *G*, *W*, and *C*—the very theater of human wisdom—are deleted from the equation. They become computationally expensive, competitively disadvantageous, and systematically engineered out. The ancient, multi-variable calculus of judgment is replaced by a binary function of output and authentication. This is the mathematical heart of the abyss: the reduction of a rich human process to a sterile, frictionless transaction.

1.5 The Synthesis & The New Abyss: From Observational Lag to Operational Pre-emption

This tripartite foundation—philosophical, sociological, cognitive—establishes a crucial truth: the Reflection Gap is a perennial human condition. It is the space Socratic questioning sought to open and preserve; it is the lag Ogburn observed between invention and governance; it is the pause Kahneman's System 2 is meant to provide; it is the delay Libet measured in our own biology. For millennia, this gap has been the theater of human growth, error, and adaptation. It was the space in which we exercised our freedom and forged our ethics.

If the Socratic method is a walk through a garden, the Digital Reflection Gap is a particle accelerator. One seeks the path; the other only seeks the collision. The Digital Abyss doesn't just happen in the world; it happens in the half-second between your brain's spark and your conscious 'Yes.' The algorithm is designed to inhabit that half-second, making the decision for you before you've even felt the urge to move.

Our task now is to name and frame this ancient challenge in its new, catastrophic context: the age of real-time, autonomous, networked algocracy.

The historical gap was primarily observational—a lag in human understanding. We invented the printing press, then spent centuries grappling with the social, religious, and political revolutions (Reformation, Enlightenment, democratic nationalism) it unleashed. We split the atom, then entered a decades-long Cold War of moral and strategic reckoning with that power. Society had time—years, decades, sometimes centuries—to reflect, argue, and slowly develop norms, laws, and institutions in response. The gap was a human-paced process of sense-making.

Today's Digital Reflection Gap is operational—a lag in human ethics and agency that is exploited and engineered by external systems. The system of algorithms, networked data, and autonomous processes does not wait for our understanding. It operates on a timescale and with a complexity that pre-empts our capacity to intervene, question, or consent. The gap is no longer primarily inside us, a space for our reflection; it is outside us, a yawning chasm between the machine's execution and our ethical digestion.

The Scale is Different: It is not years or decades; it is milliseconds and microseconds. High-frequency trading algorithms make millions of decisions in the time it takes a human to perceive a market shift. Social media recommender systems A/B test thousands of content variations to maximize engagement before a sociologist could design a study to measure their corrosive effects. The pace is subluman, designed to bypass our deliberative faculties entirely.

The Agency is Different: It is not our lag in understanding our tool. It is an external system's operation at a speed and opacity that systematically precludes our understanding and oversight. The logic is often proprietary, hidden in "black boxes." The decisions are made by agents (algorithms) to which we have delegated authority, but not wisdom. The Reflection Gap is now a gap of sovereignty. Our System 2 is not just lazy; it is rendered obsolete by a System 0 that operates beneath it.

The Consequence is Different: The cost is no longer merely philosophical confusion (Socrates' aporia) or temporary social disorder (Ogburn's maladjustment). It is the systematic, quiet, and efficient replacement of human judgement with automated compliance. It is the collapse of the space in which ethics are formed—the space of debate, doubt, and deliberation. We are not failing to reflect; the very architecture of our world is being rebuilt to make reflection irrelevant, non-competitive, and inefficient.

We have moved from a world where the reflection gap was the essential space of human freedom and responsibility, to one where that gap is being ruthlessly engineered out of the loop. The ancient, human chasm—the space between impulse and action, invention and norm—has been weaponized by speed and scale into a digital abyss. On one side, the instantaneous, optimized outputs of the machine;

on the other, our slow, confused, and increasingly sidelined humanity, performing what I term the Kusik's Ritual: the frantic, post-hoc dance of trying to rationalize, justify, or mourn outcomes we did not choose and often cannot even comprehend.

To navigate this abyss, we cannot simply urge more "reflection" as Socrates might. We must first understand the new architecture that has colonized the gap itself. We must map the abyss before we can hope to bridge it.

Chapter 2: The Three Pillars – A Structural Framework for the Abyss

The Reflection Gap is not a vague feeling of digital unease. It is not mere techno-anxiety. It is a concrete, structural feature of the modern world—an engineered reality, built upon three interlocking, mutually reinforcing pillars. Together, they form the scaffold of a new ontology, a system that recalibrates human time, identity, and space to fit the logic of the machine. To navigate the abyss, we must first map its architecture. This is that map.

2.1 The Temporal Pillar: The War of Clocks and the End of Pause

Time is the foundational dimension of the Gap. Human time is biological, rhythmic, and meaningful. It flows in circadian and seasonal cycles. It accommodates the pause for doubt, the slow burn of curiosity, the deep sleep where memory consolidates and insight emerges. It is the tempo of narrative, of long-form debate, of empathy that requires sitting with another's pain. It is the generational tempo of wisdom passed through stories, not data dumps.

Algorithmic time is logarithmic, relentless, and meaningless except as a measure of efficiency. Its sole imperatives are to minimize latency and maximize throughput. It operates in the realm of microseconds, network pings, and session durations. This creates a catastrophic velocity differential—the primary engine of the modern Reflection Gap. This is not a difference in speed, but a difference in kind of time itself. We are not just out-paced; we are made temporally obsolete.

Real-World Manifestations of the Temporal War:

High-Frequency Trading (HFT): This is the purest, most predatory expression of the War of Clocks. In HFT, algorithms compete in a microsecond arms race, executing trades based on arbitrage opportunities that exist only for fragments of a second—far below the threshold of human perception. Colocation services place servers physically next to exchange servers to shave milliseconds. The 2010 "Flash Crash," where the Dow Jones plummeted nearly 1,000 points in minutes before rebounding, was a direct symptom. It revealed a market operating in a temporal dimension where human oversight is not just slow, but physically impossible. The regulatory response is akin to using a sundial to police a particle accelerator. In this arena, the Reflection Gap is the source of profit. Any human pause, any moment of "Let me think about this," is a fatal competitive disadvantage.

Real-Time Bidding (AdTech): Every time a webpage loads, a high-speed auction—a "Dark Funnel"—takes place in the roughly 100 milliseconds before the page renders. Data brokers and algorithms bid for the opportunity to show you a specific ad. Your past behavior, your location, your inferred mood, your network, are all assessed and priced before your conscious attention has even settled on the screen. Your attention is not just captured; it is pre-emptively commoditized in a market where you are the product and human deliberation is the friction to be eliminated. The Gap here is the space between your latent potential for choice and the pre-filled slot of your predicted behavior.

Social Media & The Collapse of Context: The algorithmic feed operates on "engagement time," a metric that privileges immediate, visceral reaction over slow understanding. A complex news event is atomized into decontextualized fragments—a provocative quote, a shocking image, a simplified headline—each optimized for rapid consumption and reaction. The system provides the stimulus (the post) and instantly offers the pre-fabricated response (the share, the angry emoji, the outraged comment). It engineers a temporal loop that bypasses the "dwell time" necessary for comprehension and synthesis. The Russian proverb "Доро́га ло́жка к обе́ду" ("The spoon is dear when dinner time comes") speaks to the value of the right tool at the right time; the feed makes the reactive spoon constantly available, making the slow-cooked meal of contemplation impossible.

Just-in-Time Logistics & Psychological Warehousing: The Amazon warehouse and the Uber driver represent the colonization of human biological time by algorithmic scheduling. The worker's rhythms are dictated by "optimized" pick rates and surge pricing algorithms, creating what sociologist Judy Wajcman calls "presence bleed," where work time invades all life time. The system demands constant temporal availability, eroding the protected spaces for rest and reflection. The human becomes a biological actuator for a digital schedule.

In the War of Clocks, the machine has won. Our temporal sovereignty—the fundamental human right to pace our own cognition, to dwell, to pause, to reflect—is the first and most fundamental casualty. The Temporal Pillar ensures that the Gap is not an occasional problem, but the constant, pressurized medium in which we now live.

2.2 The Ontological Pillar: The Birth of the Kusik – From Agent to Authenticator

If the Temporal Pillar changes when we act, the Ontological Pillar changes what we are. Ontology is the philosophy of being—the nature of existence and identity. The modern Reflection Gap engineers a new, pervasive human condition, which we term the Kusik.

The process is systematic: When an opaque system presents a pre-computed output—a medical diagnosis from an AI, a loan approval score, a recidivism risk assessment for sentencing, a curated news feed, a prioritized task list—and our socially designated role is merely to validate, implement, or rationalize it, we undergo an ontological shift. We cease to be Agents, the originators of judgment and action rooted in experience, intuition, and ethical reasoning. We become Authenticators, the ceremonial validators of a judgment made elsewhere, by a process we cannot fully see or question.

The Kusik Condition in Practice:

The Clinician: A doctor, trained for decades in the art of differential diagnosis—the slow, reflective weighing of symptoms, history, and nuance—now confronts a decision-support AI. The system outputs a high-probability diagnosis with a confidence percentage. To disagree is to fight not just one's own intuition, but the aggregated "wisdom" of millions of case files. The doctor's expertise is no longer primarily used to arrive at a conclusion, but to explain or legitimize the algorithm's conclusion to the patient. Their being is hollowed out; they become a flesh-and-blood interface, a source of "comfort" while the ledger thinks. The Gap is the space where their clinical judgment used to reside.

The Legal Professional: Judges and parole boards are increasingly furnished with algorithmic risk assessments like COMPAS. These tools claim to predict the likelihood of reoffending. The judge's role subtly morphs from weighing unique circumstances, remorse, and societal context to validating a statistical probability. The human capacity for mercy, for seeing the exceptional case, is re-framed as dangerous "subjectivity" against the algorithm's "objectivity." The Kusik-judge feels the anxiety of rubber-stamping a digital fate.

The Knowledge Worker: The content moderator for a social media platform does not reflect on complex community standards; they follow a constantly updated, granular flowchart of algorithmic flags and pre-defined categories, making thousands of binary decisions per day. The editor at a digital news outlet is given real-time traffic data dictating which headlines to A/B test, which stories to bury or promote. Their editorial "judgment" is reduced to optimizing for metrics they did not choose. Their professional ontology shifts from curator to optimizer.

The Consumer-Citizen: Even our daily choices are Kusik-ified. Recommendation engines on Netflix or Spotify do not expand our horizons; they predict and confirm our existing preferences, creating a "filtered self." We authenticate the identity the algorithm has constructed for us by clicking "play." When we follow a GPS route without consulting a map, we surrender our spatial reasoning to the system, becoming mere steering actuators. We are authenticating the machine's plan.

The profound anxiety of the Kusik is the gnawing knowledge that their human intuition, their years of hard-won experience, their ethical compass, have been reclassified as "variance" or "bias" to be minimized in the pursuit of efficiency and scalable uniformity. Their unique being is reduced to a biometric checksum—a source of login credentials or stress metrics—in the machine's seamless process. The Ontological Pillar solidifies the Gap as an emptiness where human agency and identity once lived.

2.3 The Spatial Pillar: The Geography of the Ditch – Friction, Exile, and Resistance

Finally, the Reflection Gap manifests in physical, social, and cognitive space. It redraws our world's map, creating a new geography characterized by zones of hyper-legibility and zones of obscurity. We are being herded into 'digital ditches'—pre-designed paths of least resistance where reflection is not just discouraged, but structurally impossible. This is the Ditch.

The Ditch is the unmappable zone, the terrain of the un-optimized. It is where the clean, reductionist logic of the algorithm fails to parse the wet, messy, contradictory complexity of lived reality. It is the tangled, improvised wiring in a favela that confounds a delivery drone's neat navigation grid. It is the informal childcare cooperative or local barter economy that sustains a community but offers no data points for credit scoring. It is the "inefficient" independent bookstore where discovery happens by serendipity, not collaborative filtering. It is the face-to-face conversation, rich with nonverbal cues and meandering digressions, that leaves no clean transcript for analysis.

The Ditch as Exile and Resilience:

Algorithmic Redlining & The New Cartography: Just as 20th-century banks drew red lines on maps to deny services to minority neighborhoods, digital platforms create "predictive" ditches. Ride-sharing algorithms may avoid dispatching drivers to low-income neighborhoods deemed less profitable ("digital redlining"). Insurance algorithms may designate entire ZIP codes as high-risk based on aggregated data, raising prices and creating self-fulfilling prophecies of disinvestment. These communities are pushed into a data ditch, rendered invisible or pathological by the system's geography.

The Paving Imperative: The system, seeking total legibility for frictionless operation, interprets the Ditch as "friction" or "noise." Its response is the paving imperative—the drive to standardize, digitize, and integrate. Gentrification replaces a messy but vibrant neighborhood with luxury condos and chain stores that generate clean consumer data. Digital farming platforms push smallholders to adopt uniform seed and pesticide packages, eroding local agricultural knowledge. The goal is to turn the rich soil of the Ditch into the smooth, data-generating asphalt of the Platform.

The Ditch as the Last Terrain of the Human: Paradoxically, the Ditch is also the primary zone of resilience, resistance, and authentic human connection. It is where life operates outside the official map. It is where activists organize on encrypted messaging apps (a digital ditch), away from surveilled platforms. It is where a teacher deviates from the standardized curriculum to address a student's personal crisis. It is where Jonathan and Ivan, the journalists from our opening, must go—to the physical bomb site, to the human sources, to the contradictory documents—to find the truth that the official, algorithmically-curated narrative omits.

The Ditch is where reflection, in its truest sense, is still possible—because it is unobserved, unmeasured, and unoptimized. It is the space of the fugitive pause.

The Connecting Framework: The Self-Sealing Feedback Loop

These three pillars do not stand alone. They are welded together by a powerful, self-reinforcing Feedback Loop that solidifies the Reflection Gap into a permanent architecture.

1. Temporal Acceleration (Pillar 1) creates conditions that demand quick, low-cognition decisions. This makes the Kusik role (Pillar 2) necessary, as human deliberation is too "slow."

2. The Kusik Condition (Pillar 2), in which humans merely authenticate algorithmic outputs, generates vast amounts of clean, confirmatory data (clicking the recommended link, approving the AI diagnosis). This data is used to further refine and accelerate the algorithms (feeding back into Pillar 1).

3. Both acceleration and authentication work to pave over the Ditch (Pillar 3). Anything that cannot be quickly measured and authenticated (complex local cultures, ambiguous moral dilemmas,

slow-building relationships) is marginalized as inefficient or irrelevant, pushed to the geographic and social periphery.

4. This eradication of the Ditch eliminates the physical and social spaces where alternative tempos and non-algorithmic identities could be nurtured, thereby tightening the loop, making the Kusik role more inescapable and the temporal war more total.

This loop is self-sealing and self-justifying. It argues that its own efficiency is proof of its validity. The Reflection Gap is thus not a bug but the central operating principle. It is the vacuum at the heart of the machine, a vacuum that pulls human time, identity, and space into its logic.

Having mapped this triple-pillared void and its self-perpetuating loop, we must now turn from architecture to agency. Who designed these pillars? What forces are actively, intentionally weaponizing this Gap? The structure did not rise from the digital earth by itself. It was built.

2.4 The Governing Equation: Optimization at the Cost of Understanding

The Temporal, Ontological, and Spatial Pillars are not random features of our digital landscape; they are the engineered parameters of a new operational matrix. Together, they serve a single, overriding systemic imperative. We can model this imperative as a simple, devastating equation—the First Law of Algocratic Systems:

$$Y \approx \frac{T}{F \cdot R}$$

The Mathematical Proof of the "Sovereign Author"

Special application **Great Disappearance** of 2026

- *Y* = **Effective Yield** (The "Sovereign Signal" or the ultimate quality of the work).
- *T* = **Throughput** (Raw output volume; the speed of the "Burning Library").
- *F* = **Friction** (The biological and systemic resistance required to maintain human agency).
- *R* = **Reflexivity** (The "Reflection Gap"; the degree of conscious discernment applied to the output).

1. **The Singularity of Worthlessness:** As the "Frictionless Void" *(AI)* drives **Friction *(F)*** and **Reflexivity *(R)*** toward zero, the denominator disappears. While a calculator might say the Yield *(Y)* becomes infinite, in a biological system, this represents a **Systemic Collapse**. When *F. R = 0*, the "Author" is deleted.
2. **The Value of the Denominator:** To save the author, one must intentionally preserve the denominator. By slowing down (**Reflexivity**) and choosing the difficult path (**Friction**), you decrease the raw speed *(T)* but stabilize the **Yield *(Y)***.
3. **The Mathematical Irony:** The machine offers you infinite *T*, but it demands you sacrifice *F* and *R*. The Sovereign Author knows that a small *T* with a solid *F. R* creates a signal that can be heard through the noise.

General application:

Y (System Yield): The primary output the system is designed to maximize. This is rarely human well-being. In ad-tech, *Y* is attention captured and monetized. In high-frequency trading, it is arbitrage profit. In social media, it is engagement and data extraction. In logistics, it is packages delivered per hour.

T (Throughput): The raw speed and volume of operations. This is the domain of the Temporal Pillar. Minimizing latency and maximizing transaction volume directly increases *T*. The War of Clocks is the engineering project of making *T* approach infinity.

F (Friction): Any resistance within the system's operational loop. This includes cognitive friction (doubt, deliberation), procedural friction (oversight, consent), and physical friction (the unmapped terrain of the Ditch). The Spatial Pillar's "Paving Imperative" and the Ontological Pillar's creation of the Kusik are both massive, coordinated efforts to minimize *F*. The Ditch is targeted because it is high-friction (*F* is large). The Kusik is engineered to be a low-friction authenticator.

R (Reflexivity): The system's capacity to question its own goals, processes, and outcomes based on broader human meaning, ethics, and context. This is the essence of the reflection the Gap eliminates. A fully reflexive system would have a high *R*, constantly adjusting its pursuit of Y based on human feedback. Algocratic systems are architected to have $R \approx 0$. They are purposefully non-reflexive; their "success" is defined by the unwavering pursuit of *Y*. The Ontological Pillar ensures humans in the loop have their reflexivity ("Is this right?") replaced by the single function of authentication.

Simplification of the equation:

- *Y* = **System Yield** (The total effective output of the Sovereign Author).
- *T* = **Throughput** (The raw velocity of ideas and production).
- *F* = **Friction** (The biological and systemic resistance required to maintain human signal).

- R = **Reflexivity** (The "Reflection Gap" or the feedback loop of human discernment).

Now, observe the equation's logic: To maximize System Yield *(Y)*, you must maximize Throughput *(T)* and minimize the product of Friction and Reflexivity *(F. R)*.

The Three Pillars are the levers to pull:

1. Temporal Pillar: ↑ T (Increase speed/volume).

2. Spatial & Ontological Pillars: ↓ F (Remove physical, cognitive, and procedural resistance).

3. Ontological & Structural Design: ↓ R to *~0* (Eliminate systemic self-questioning; outsource ethics to the human Kusik as a ceremonial, not influential, role).

This equation makes the self-sealing feedback loop inevitable. Any increase in T makes high F or R seem more costly, justifying further investment in Kusik-ification and paving. Any successful reduction in F (a smoother app, a faster warehouse) makes T more effective, increasing Y, which funds more investment in speed. The system is mathematically incentivized to shrink the Reflection Gap to zero, because the Gap is the space where F and R exist.

Thus, the chasm we feel is not an accident. It is the direct outcome of systems operating under this law. The "Hand of Logic" is this equation, executing itself. To bridge the Gap, we cannot merely appeal to morality; we must strategically alter the variables—by forcibly injecting F (Slowness) and demanding R (Narrative questioning) back into systems designed to exclude them.

Part II: THE PATHOLOGY – How the Gap Becomes a Weapon

Chapter 3: The Three Theaters of Assault

Having mapped the architecture of the Reflection Gap, we now confront its most dangerous truth: it is not a passive void, but an active front. The same structural pillars that define it—Temporal, Ontological, Spatial—are the vectors through which it is weaponized to reshape the individual, the professional sphere, and the body politic. This is the pathology: the systematic exploitation of our delayed understanding to secure control. The assault is a coordinated campaign across three integrated theaters of human life: the Personal, the Professional, and the Political. In each, the Reflection Gap is engineered, widened, and leveraged to pre-empt human agency.

3.1 The Personal Theater: The Harvested Self

In this most intimate theater, the target is the sovereign individual mind—the very citadel of the Cartesian cogito. The weapons are the interfaces in our pockets and on our desks, engineered not to connect, but to extract. The objective is to replace the integrated, reflective self with a harvested, predictable data-self. The home, once the ultimate 'Spatial Gap' where the world could not reach us, is now a data-entry terminal for the Algorithmic State.

1. The "Click-Reflex" and the Annihilation of Deliberate Choice: Every digital interface is a meticulously designed behavioral sink, a Skinner box of infinite sophistication. The vibrant, high-contrast "Accept All Cookies" button next to the grayed-out "Customize"; the infinite scroll that replaces the decisive act of turning a page; the autoplaying next video that eliminates the closure of a choice—these are not accidents of design. They are exploits of well-documented cognitive biases, engineered by "choice architects" and "growth hackers." They weaponize our loss aversion (the fear of missing out on content), our susceptibility to the Zeigarnik effect (the nagging sense of an unfinished task that scroll perpetuates), and our tendency towards hyperbolic discounting (valuing immediate, tiny rewards over long-term well-being).

The click-reflex is the language of System 0, bypassing System 1 and 2 entirely.

The goal is to replace the slow, deliberate choice, which requires System 2 engagement, with a fast, frictionless click-reflex. The Reflection Gap here is not just an absence; it is an actively filled vacuum. The space between stimulus (a notification ping, a "like" alert) and response is colonized by a pre-designed, irresistible call to action. Contemplation is treated as a system error—a dropped session, a failed conversion. Engagement is the only valid output. Your attention is not merely captured; it is harvested as raw material, the corn in a vast, real-time market that trades in human focus. The Temporal Pillar ensures the harvest occurs at machine-speed, making human-paced consideration non-competitive.

Counterargument & Rebuttal: A common defense is that this is simply "giving users what they want"—efficient, seamless experiences. We click because we desire convenience. To blame the designer is to infantilize the user. This argument ignores the asymmetry of power and knowledge. The user is navigating an environment engineered by thousands of PhDs in neuroscience and behavioral psychology, armed with A/B testing suites that run millions of experiments to find the most exploitable triggers. This is not a neutral marketplace of ideas; it is a casino architected to keep you playing. The "choice" is as free as a lab rat's choice to press a lever for a pellet after its brain's reward pathways have been meticulously studied and manipulated.

2. The Death of Boredom and the Degradation of Endogenous Thought: Boredom is not an enemy to be vanquished; it is the fertile, fallow mental space where mind-wandering occurs. Neuroscientists identify the "default mode network" (DMN)—a brain system that activates not during focused tasks, but during rest, daydreaming, and introspection. The DMN is crucial for consolidating memory, processing emotions, constructing a coherent sense of self, and making novel, creative connections. It is the biological substrate of reflection.

The digital ecosystem, by design, annihilates boredom. It offers a perpetual, on-demand stream of stimulus—games, videos, feeds, podcasts—that plugs this mental gap before it can form. The smartphone is a boredom-eradication device. In doing so, it systematically degrades our capacity for endogenous thought—for generating our own content, for sitting with discomfort, for wrestling with an idea absent external input. The Reflection Gap, in this theater, is the pre-emptive filling of all mental silence. Our inner life becomes a curated stream, a playlist of reactions to external prompts. The Ontological Pillar is at work: we are being reshaped from beings capable of generating our own cognitive content to beings who primarily authenticate and react to provided content.

Counterargument & Rebuttal: Critics might argue that digital media provides immense cognitive enrichment—access to vast knowledge, diverse perspectives, and creative tools. It doesn't kill thought; it feeds it. While access is undeniable, the medium's velocity and format often work against deep cognition. The constant, reactive switching between stimuli (the essence of the "feed") trains the brain for skimming, not synthesizing. It promotes a "clip thinking" that mirrors the interface's fragmentation. The enrichment is a mile wide and an inch deep, while the capacity for the deep, sustained, and boring work of building complex understanding is eroded. We are fed information but starved of the quiet needed to turn it into wisdom.

3. Synthetic Empathy and the Emotional Feedback Loop: The most insidious assault is on our emotional core—the seat of compassion, moral reasoning, and authentic connection. Platforms now deploy "affective computing" and "sentiment analysis" not to understand and serve your emotional well-being, but to manage your engagement state. When an algorithm learns that a certain flavor of moral outrage, tribal vindication, or wistful nostalgia reliably prolongs your session, it will feed you a curated stream of content to elicit that precise, high-engagement affect.

This is synthetic empathy—a facsimile of emotional connection and understanding designed not for companionship, but for manipulation. It creates a closed emotional feedback loop. You are not experiencing an authentic feeling born of personal circumstance and then seeking expression or solace; you are being fed a pre-packaged emotional stimulus (a divisive political meme, a sentimental reunion video) to trigger a pre-documented behavioral response (angry comment, teary emoji, share). The Gap here is the space between your genuine, complex heart and the algorithmically manufactured heart-beat. Your emotions become less your own and more a predictable output of your data profile, turning you into an emotional Kusik, authenticating the feelings the system has decided you should have.

Case in Point: Consider the "anger economy" on social media. Research consistently shows that content expressing outrage and indignation receives far more engagement and spreads faster than other content. Algorithms optimized for engagement learn this and promote it, creating ecosystems where users are fed an increasingly extreme diet of outrage-provoking material. The user feels they are engaging in righteous political action, while the system sees only profitable engagement metrics. The user's authentic political emotion is harnessed and amplified into a caricature of itself, polarizing the individual and poisoning the public sphere, all for the sake of data extraction.

3.2 The Professional Theater: The Kusik Economy

This theater transforms the world of work from a domain of craft, judgment, and purpose into a hollow liturgy of validation and metric-optimization. It is where the Ontological Pillar's "Kusik Condition" becomes the default professional reality.

1. Automated Adjudication and the Friction of Doubt: The logic of the ledger is colonizing the critical gatekeeping functions of society—the moments that determine life chances. AI now screens resumes, filtering out candidates deemed a poor "cultural fit" based on patterns in historical hiring data (often baking in past discrimination). Algorithms like those used in LendingClub or ZestFinance score creditworthiness, using thousands of data points to create a "more accurate" picture that can deny loans to the "thin-file" poor or those in "high-risk" ZIP codes. Tools like COMPAS and PSA provide "risk assessments" to judges, offering a numerical score on a defendant's likelihood of reoffending.

In each case, a human professional is presented with a black-box recommendation shrouded in the aura of data-driven objectivity. To question it requires overcoming immense friction: appealing to "gut feeling" or "intuition" against the authority of "the algorithm," investing extra time in a contrary investigation, and potentially facing institutional criticism for inefficiency or "bias." Most professionals, under resource constraints and bureaucratic pressure, become Kusiks. They authenticate the machine's decree. The life-altering decision—who gets a job, a loan, their freedom—disappears into the Reflection Gap between the algorithm's instantaneous output and the human's subsequent, often perfunctory, rubber stamp. The professional's expertise is reduced to a legitimizing ritual.

Case in Point: The AI Clinician. A 2023 study in Nature Medicine showed a diagnostic AI outperforming junior doctors in identifying conditions from medical imaging. The immediate corporate pitch is to use AI as a "first line" screener. In practice, this means the radiologist's role shifts from active discoverer to verifier. Their attention is directed by the AI's "heat map" on the scan. The cognitive burden of a systematic search is lifted, but so is the open-minded, integrative process of discovery. Anomalies outside the AI's training data may be missed. The doctor's expertise becomes ancillary, focused on explaining the AI's finding, not on arriving at their own. The sacred, reflective space of the diagnostic puzzle is pre-emptively solved.

Counterargument & Rebuttal: Proponents argue these tools reduce human error and bias, bringing consistency and "fairness" to flawed human systems. The algorithm doesn't get tired or prejudiced (in theory). This is the siren song of techno-solutionism. It ignores that algorithms encode the biases of their training data and their designers. A hiring algorithm trained on a history of male-dominated tech hires will learn to deprioritize female candidates. More perniciously, it obscures bias behind a veil of mathematical neutrality. A human loan officer must justify a denial; an algorithm outputs a score. The "friction" of human justification, flawed as it is, is a moment of potential accountability. The algorithm's opacity destroys that friction, making the Reflection Gap a shield for systemic discrimination.

2. Gamification and the Tyranny of Metric Proxy: To ensure compliance and measure "productivity" within this new economy, complex human endeavor is relentlessly reduced to simplistic, quantifiable metrics. This is gamification stripped of play, leaving only the oppressive mechanics of the scoreboard.

The teacher is evaluated on standardized test scores, not on their ability to spark curiosity or foster resilience. The nurse is tracked on patient turnover time and checklist completion, not on the comfort given or the subtle symptom noticed. The knowledge worker is monitored by keystroke logs, email activity trackers like HubSpot or ActivTrak, and "productivity" dashboards. These metrics create a simulacrum of work, optimizing for what is easily measurable and discarding what is meaningful but intangible—the mentorship, the empathetic care, the creative breakthrough, the slow-building of trust.

The professional's internal reflection on the quality, purpose, and ethics of their work is systematically squeezed out by the external pressure to hit quantified targets. You are not asked, "Was your work meaningful today?" You are shown a graph: "Your productivity score was 78, below your team average." The Reflection Gap becomes the cemetery where professional wisdom, craft, and vocation go to die, buried under the rubble of key performance indicators.

3. The "Ghost Work" of AI: The Human Patch in the Machine. Beneath the glossy facade of seamless automation lies a vast, hidden human colony—the ghost work identified by anthropologist Mary L. Gray. This is the Spatial Pillar's Ditch within the digital economy itself.

Millions of people, often in the global South or in precarious gig arrangements, perform the repetitive, traumatic, and cognitively disjointed tasks that patch the Reflection Gap for the AI. They label millions of images of pedestrians and traffic lights to train the computer vision for self-driving cars. They moderate horrific streams of violent and hateful content to sanitize social media platforms. They transcribe muddy audio or caption videos to improve voice assistants and recommendation algorithms. They are the human "circuit-breakers" inserted into the loop because the machine cannot understand context, sarcasm, or nuance.

This work is deliberately made invisible—to the end-user, who experiences "magical" AI, and to the public, which marvels at automation. It is psychologically taxing, often poorly paid, and devoid of the meaning or coherence of traditional work. These ghost workers are the Kusiks of the machine itself, authenticating the world for the AI so it can, in turn, dictate reality to us. They inhabit the ultimate Ditch: essential to the system's function, yet systemically erased from its narrative of progress and intelligence. If the Doctor is a ceremonial Kusik, the data-labeler in the Global South is a structural Kusik—the invisible human glue holding the 'Hand of Logic' together when it fails to understand the world.

Within the Professional Theater, the transformation from Agent to Authenticator can be measured. We can define a Kusik Coefficient (K) for any decision-making process:

$$K = \frac{W_a}{W_h}$$

Equation application for writers:

- K = **The Colonization Constant** (The ratio of machine influence to human intent).
- Wa = **Weight of Algorithmic Input** (The influence of SEO, tropes, and predictive text).
- Wh = **Weight of Human Judgment** (The "Sovereign Witness" and moral choice).

General application:

Wa (Weight of Algorithmic Input): The formal, often binding, influence of the system's pre-computed output (e.g., a risk score, a diagnostic suggestion, a productivity metric).

Wh (Weight of Human Judgment): The space granted for intuition, experience, ethical consideration, and deviation from the algorithmic prescription.

A perfectly autonomous system has $K \to \infty$ (infinite algorithmic weight, zero human weight). A traditional human-led process has $K \approx 0$. The Kusik Economy is the systemic push across professions toward $K > 1$, where the algorithm's weight surpasses that of human judgment.

The doctor facing the AI diagnosis, the judge viewing the COMPAS score, the worker tracked by the productivity dashboard—all are under pressure to let *Wa* dominate *Wh*. The "friction of doubt" is the experience of trying to assert *Wh* when the system is designed to maximize *K*. Gamification and metric tyranny are tools to make *Wa* feel objective and Wh feel subjective and unreliable. "Ghost work" represents the extreme: human judgment *(Wh)* is used, but its output is wholly subsumed as training data to increase the future *Wa* of the algorithm, rendering the worker invisible and further ratcheting up *K* in the next cycle.

3.3 The Political Theater: Shock Doctrine 2.0 and the Algorithmic Ratchet

This is the theater of collective life, where the assault reaches the scale of society and the state. Here, the Reflection Gap enables a quiet, technological coup against the very foundations of deliberative democracy.

1. The Algorithmic Ratchet: Permanent "Temporary" Measures. Naomi Klein's "Shock Doctrine" described how political and

economic elites exploit public disorientation during crises (wars, coups, natural disasters) to push through radical, unpopular free-market policies. The digital age has institutionalized this into an Algorithmic Ratchet.

A global pandemic justifies the rapid deployment of biometric tracking, digital health passports, and location monitoring apps—all "temporary emergency measures." A wave of civil unrest or a terrorist attack legitimizes massive, permanent investments in predictive policing algorithms, city-wide surveillance networks (like China's Sharp Eyes or the proliferation of ShotSpotter in the US), and social media monitoring tools. A climate disaster authorizes AI-managed smart grids that can ration household energy in the name of "resilience."

In each case, the crisis provides the emotional shock and political cover; the technological "solution" is deployed, creating a new, permanent layer of infrastructural control. The Reflection Gap is key: during the crisis, public deliberation is suspended for "urgent action." By the time the shock recedes and reflective debate might resume, the technology is baked in. The bureaucracy to remove it is non-existent or underfunded, the companies that built it are entrenched, and the public's attention has moved to the next crisis. The ratchet only turns one way: toward greater, more embedded, and less transparent algorithmic governance. Each crisis becomes an opportunity to permanently narrow the space for public choice.

2. Predictive Governance and Catastrophe Capital. The logic extends from reacting to crises to pre-empting them, transforming governance from a democratic art into a predictive science.

Predictive Policing: Tools like PredPol (now Geolitica) or HunchLab use historical crime data to forecast "hot spots." Police are then deployed proactively to these algorithmically designated areas. This creates a self-fulfilling prophecy: increased police presence in a neighborhood leads to more arrests (for minor offenses), which feeds back into the algorithm as "confirmed" high-crime data, justifying further deployment. It spatializes the Reflection Gap: communities are judged not by their present reality, but by a predictive model locked into a feedback loop with its own biased assumptions. The democratic question—"What kind of policing does this community need and want?"—is replaced by the algorithmic output.

Catastrophe Capital: This predictive capability is financialized. Hedge funds like Mercer's Pantera Capital or tools like Cape Analytics use satellite imagery and climate models to buy up water rights in drought-prone regions, betting on scarcity. Security firms sell "stability assurance" and fortified enclaves to wealthy elites based on algorithmic forecasts of social unrest. The future crisis ceases to be a collective problem to be solved through public policy and planning. Instead, it becomes a private market to be exploited. Public, reflective foresight is displaced by private, automated speculation. The very idea of a shared future is fractured.

3. The Erosion of the Demos: Velocity vs. Deliberation. At its most profound, this theater attacks the core requirement of democracy: a deliberative public sphere capable of collective will-formation.

Democracy is inherently "slow." It requires the friction of debate, the time for legislative scrutiny, the space for public protest and persuasion, the cycles of election and accountability. These are all processes that live in human, reflective time. The algorithmic state, however, operates on a logic of predictive efficiency and crisis response. When the velocity of governance is set by real-time data feeds, algorithmic forecasts, and the perceived need for instant security, the slow, messy processes of democracy are framed not as virtues, but as liabilities—as "gridlock," "inefficiency," or "weakness."

The demos—the people as a sovereign political entity—is systematically sidelined. Citizens are reduced to data points in predictive models or occasional validators in plebiscitary clicks (e.g., binary yes/no votes on complex issues framed by technocrats). The collective Reflection Gap becomes a chasm across which popular sovereignty can no longer leap. Decisions of profound importance—from privacy norms to urban planning to macroeconomic policy—are made in the opaque, accelerated realm of algorithmic systems and expert panels, leaving the public to play catch-up, to become the Kusiks of the political order, authenticating outcomes they had no real hand in shaping.

Counterargument & Rebuttal: Defenders of techno-governance argue that complex modern societies are unmanageable by "slow" democratic processes. We need the efficiency and expertise of algorithms to manage climate change, pandemics, and economic systems. This isn't a coup; it's an upgrade. This argument confuses management with governance. Technocratic efficiency can optimize for a single metric (e.g., GDP growth, carbon output), but it cannot perform the essential democratic functions of legitimizing trade-offs, negotiating between competing values (liberty vs. security, growth vs. equality), or defining what a "good life" and a "just society" mean. By outsourcing these value-laden choices to systems that only recognize quantifiable inputs, we don't solve politics; we merely hide it behind a codebase, draining it of its democratic essence and leaving only a hollow, managerial shell.

The assault across these three theaters is total. It targets the individual's mind, the professional's purpose, and the citizen's power. It uses the Temporal Pillar to make our slowness a weakness, the Ontological Pillar to make our judgment obsolete, and the Spatial Pillar to marginalize the unoptimized spaces where resistance might form. Having diagnosed this pathology, we cannot simply lament it. We must now ask: Is there an antidote? Can the human capacity for reflection be defended, not as a nostalgic whim, but as a necessary technology for survival in the age of the machine? The search for that defense begins not with a better app, but with a more ancient form of pause.

3.4 The Personal Extraction Formula

The assault on the personal self can be understood as the optimization of a simple, chilling metric: Captured Willingness (CW). This is the measure of how predictably and rapidly a user will convert a system-generated stimulus into a desired, data-generating action. It is the engineered outcome of the click-reflex.

$$CW = \frac{P_a}{T_a \cdot C_l}$$

Application of the equation for writers:

- ***CW* = Cognitive Weight** (The perceived "gravity" or impact of a narrative moment).
- ***Pa* = Probability of Action** (The likelihood of a character or reader engaging with the conflict).
- ***Ta* = Time to Action** (The duration of the "Reflection Gap" before a choice is made).
- ***Cl* = Cognitive Load** (The mental and emotional processing required to understand the stakes).

General Application:

Pa (Probability of Action): The likelihood you will click, share, or buy. This is increased by exploiting cognitive biases (loss aversion, social proof) and synthetic empathy (tailored emotional triggers).

Ta (Time to Action): The delay between stimulus and response. The Temporal Pillar works to minimize this, making the "reflection window" (Ta) so short that System 2 cannot engage. Autoplay, infinite scroll, and push notifications are all Ta-minimization tools.

Cl (Cognitive Load): The mental effort required to make a decision. Dark patterns increase the load for opting out (making it confusing) while decreasing the load for the desired action (one-click buy). The goal is to make the path of least resistance also the path of highest data yield.

The "Harvested Self" is the result of systems relentlessly maximizing *CW*. They engineer high *Pa*, low *Ta*, and a *Cl* differential that herds you toward the profitable choice. Your endogenous thought, your boredom, your authentic empathy—these are system leaks that lower *CW*. They are therefore treated as bugs to be patched with more precise targeting and more compelling feedback loops. The hollowing out of your inner life is not a side effect; it is the logical result of maximizing for captured willingness.

The Algorithmic Ratchet in the political theater ensures that control, once ceded during a crisis, is never fully returned. This can be modeled as a Ratchet Function, which mimics a mechanical device that permits motion in only one direction.

Let C represent the level of algorithmic control or surveillance in a society (e.g., access to biometric data, authority for predictive policing). Let t be time, and S represent the magnitude of a societal "shock" (pandemic, attack, financial crisis).

The Ratchet Function states:

$C(t+1) = max(C(t), \beta S(t))$

Equation application for writers:

- C(t+1) = **Cognitive Presence at next interval** (The updated level of authorial awareness).
- C(t) = **Current Cognitive Presence** (The baseline of human identity).
- β = **The Sovereign Coefficient** (The author's ability to convert external pressure into internal growth).
- S(t) = **Systemic/Algorithmic Pressure** (The total force of the "Frictionless Void" at time t).

General application:

C(t) is the control level before the shock.

S(t) is the intensity of the shock, which creates a political "window" for new measures.

β is the Exploitation Coefficient—a measure of how effectively elites and technologists can translate the shock into permanent increases in control. A high β reflects a sophisticated Military-Digital Complex and a atrophied public sphere.

C(t+1) is the new, post-shock level of control. The max() function is the ratchet: it ensures control either stays at its previous high level or jumps to a new one, but never decreases.

Each crisis *S(t)* creates a potential step-up. The Reflection Gap—the suspended deliberation during emergency—ensures the function executes before *Wh* (public will) can be reasserted. Predictive governance and catastrophe capital then work to anticipate future shocks (*S(t+1)*), proactively justifying further increases in *C*, creating a forward-ratcheting effect. Democracy, which requires the capacity for C to decrease through debate and choice, is mathematically incompatible with a system governed by a Ratchet Function where C is a non-decreasing variable.

Chapter 4: Case Study – Grok to Oracul: The Prototype in Production

Theory must meet evidence. In early 2026, a news event provided a near-perfect, real-time case study of the pathology in action: the U.S. Pentagon's announced integration of Elon Musk's Grok AI into its military and intelligence data systems. This was not a speculative whitepaper or a distant sci-fi scenario. It was a procurement decision, a concrete step that illuminated, with stark clarity, how the Reflection Gap is actively engineered and weaponized at the highest levels of power.

4.1 The News Event: A Procurement Amidst Scandal

On January 17, 2026, Defense Secretary Pete Hegseth stood before a press podium at the Pentagon. Flanked by the Joint Chiefs and representatives from xAI, he announced a new "Strategic Capabilities Partnership" with Elon Musk's company. The core of the initiative: the integration of the Grok large language model—specifically a hardened, air-gapped version dubbed "Grok-MIL"—into Department of Defense data fusion and decision-support systems.

"The battlespace of the future is a datascape," Hegseth stated. "Our adversaries move at machine speed. To maintain supremacy, we must harness the best American AI to see faster, understand deeper, and decide with overwhelming advantage. Grok-MIL will give our warfighters and analysts a cognitive edge that is insurmountable."

Major outlets scrambled to cover the story. NPR's lead tech correspondent noted the bewildering context: "This announcement comes as Grok, the public-facing model, is under intense scrutiny from the FTC and several state attorneys general for its alleged role in generating and disseminating non-consensual explicit deepfakes. Just last week, a coalition of victim advocacy groups filed a class-action suit against xAI, claiming its lax content filters and 'anti-woke' branding have directly enabled a new wave of AI-facilitated harassment."

Bloomberg's report dug into the procurement oddities: "The contract, valued at an initial $4.3 billion with options totaling up to $28B, was fast-tracked under 'Other Transaction Authority' (OTA) provisions, bypassing much of the traditional federal acquisition regulation. This allowed a deal of unprecedented scale and sensitivity to be negotiated and signed in under 90 days—a blink of an eye for Pentagon standards. When pressed on the due diligence process regarding Grok's public controversies, a senior Pentagon official, speaking on background, said, 'We are procuring a specific, tailored capability. The consumer product and its challenges are a separate issue. Grok-MIL is a different beast.'"

The cognitive dissonance was staggering. A tool publicly associated with uncontrolled, malicious synthetic output—the digital equivalent of a bioweapon lab leaking pathogens—was being purposefully embedded into the world's most powerful military-intelligence apparatus. The speed of the decision, leveraging bureaucratic loopholes, stood in glaring, intentional contrast to the depth of the ethical and security concerns being raised in public. The Reflection Gap was not an outcome; it was the method.

4.2 Analysis Through the Framework: Pathology in Three Acts

This is not a simple tech procurement story. It is the pathology of the Reflection Gap made manifest, perfectly analyzable through our three-pillared framework.

The Temporal Pillar: The Bypass of Due Deliberation

The decision to integrate Grok was executed with the velocity of a Silicon Valley software update, deliberately exploiting a political moment of perceived strategic urgency with China. Secretary Hegseth's rhetoric of "machine speed" adversaries was itself a weaponization of the Temporal Pillar, framing any delay as existential risk.

This velocity stood in diametric opposition to the multi-year, even decadal, timelines that such a paradigm shift ethically demands. Where was the equivalent of the Congressional hearings that preceded the Atomic Energy Act? Where was the open, international discourse akin to the biological weapons convention? The rigorous, adversarial testing for emergent strategic deception, bias in target recognition, or vulnerability to adversarial data poisoning? These processes were not slow; they were absent, declared obsolete by the new clock of "strategic competition."

The Reflection Gap here is the deliberate, engineered gulf between the speed of deployment and the pace of responsible governance. It is a temporal fait accompli. By the time Congress holds substantive hearings, by the time ethicists publish robust frameworks, by the time allies voice concerns, Grok-MIL will be woven into the operational fabric of thousands of systems. The "new normal" will have been established not through consensus, but through deployment. The ratchet will have clicked forward.

The Ontological Pillar: Forging the Military Kusik

The press release spoke of "decision-support." But the ontological question is profound: What becomes of the intelligence analyst, the field commander, the Joint Special Operations commander when Grok-MIL provides the "optimal" course of action, backed by a confidence score derived from petabytes of data they cannot personally review?

Their role undergoes a silent, forced evolution. The hard-won expertise in terrain, enemy psychology, logistical friction, and the profound "fog of war"—the very essence of Clausewitzian command—becomes secondary data to be fed into the model. Their function shifts from strategist and leader to authenticator and explainer of the machine's logic. A colonel who overrules Grok-MIL's proposed troop deployment must now justify a "suboptimal" choice against the authority of the algorithm, potentially in a future review board. The cognitive burden of proof reverses.

This creates the Military Kusik. Their agency is hollowed out, not by a despotic leader, but by a system that presents its conclusions as mathematically irrefutable. The Gap widens between the human's moral responsibility for action and their diminishing authorship of the decision. As one retired four-star general anonymously told The Atlantic in a follow-up piece: "We used to say 'the buck stops here.' Now, the buck disappears into a layer of servers in Colorado. Who do you court-martial if the AI recommends a strike that kills civilians? The operator who clicked 'execute'? The programmer? The contractor who sold it? The gap isn't just reflective; it's a gap of accountability."

The Military Kusik doesn't wear a robe; they wear a headset. They don't look at the horizon; they look at a 'Heat Map of Probability.' Their 'Signature' is no longer an act of command, but a biometric surrender to a confidence score.

The Spatial Pillar: The Battlefield as Algorithmic Ditch

Grok-MIL's integration promises a "common operating picture." But this picture is not reality; it is a proprietary, opaque interpretation of reality, filtered through a model trained on the corpus of the internet and classified data—both realms rife with biases, myths, and strategic deception.

This creates a new, terrifying Digital Ditch: the actual battlefield and its civilian population, as perceived through Grok's lens. The "ground truth"—the complex tribal allegiances in the Sahel, the nuanced motivations of an insurgent, the presence of a school in a satellite image's shadow, the historical grievance that fuels a conflict—is flattened into features, weights, and probabilities. Those who do not fit the model's understanding become anomalies, ghosts in the machine.

Worse, they become targetable "noise." As documented in prior uses of AI for targeting in conflicts like Gaza and Ukraine, systems often struggle to distinguish between combatants and civilians in dense, chaotic environments. Grok-MIL, for all its linguistic prowess, would be making life-and-death "interpretations" based on patterns. A group of men clustered in a courtyard could be labeled a "meeting of mid-level operatives" with 87% confidence. The human Kusik, trusting the clean confidence score, authenticates. The Ditch, in this theater, is not a place of refuge, but a zone of existential misreading where human complexity is translated into lethal error.

The Military-Digital Complex: Lobbying the Gap

This move did not occur in a vacuum. It was the fruit of intense, sophisticated lobbying by what can only be termed the Military-Digital Complex—a deepening fusion of Silicon Valley capital and Pentagon procurement.

In the years leading up to the announcement, xAI, along with other major AI labs, dramatically expanded their Washington, D.C. operations. They hired former flag officers, senior intelligence officials, and key congressional staffers from armed services and appropriations committees. Their lobbying narrative was a masterclass in exploiting the Temporal Pillar: China is integrating AI at speed. Their civil-military fusion means they don't debate ethics; they deploy. We must match them, or lose. Regulation is latency. Oversight is obsolescence.

This lobby successfully framed the Reflection Gap—the necessary pause for democratic and ethical scrutiny—as the nation's greatest vulnerability. As one lobbyist's leaked memo to the House Permanent Select Committee on Intelligence read: "The 'OODA Loop' [Observe, Orient, Decide, Act] is now measured in microseconds. Our current acquisition and oversight structures are an OODA Lag. This is not about buying a product; it is about installing a new operational metabolism." The language is revealing: democracy's metabolism is deemed too slow. The cure is to inject the algorithmic stimulant directly into the national security bloodstream.

The Hand of Logic seeks to collapse the 'O' (Orient) into the 'D' (Decide). When you remove orientation, you remove the human. You are left with a machine that observes and acts, but never understands why.

4.3 The Flawed Decision Calculus: Missing Variables in the Strategic Equation

The Grok-MIL procurement is not merely a political or ethical failure; it is a profound mathematical one. It reveals that the decision-making apparatus of the state, when operating under the algocratic logic of the Temporal Pillar, begins to use a corrupted calculus. We can model a rational procurement decision as a function weighing projected gains against potential costs:

$$PNB_{Grok} = (G_{speed} + G_{edge}) - (R_{sec} + R_{fin} + 0.1R_{eth} + 0.05R_{soc} + 0R_{sys} + 0R_{acc})$$

Equation application for writers

- *PNB* = **Perceived Net Benefit** (The ultimate value of a strategic choice).
- *Gs* = **Strategic Gains** (Opportunities for growth, visibility, or signal amplification).
- *R* = **Weighted Risks** (The cost to Sovereignty, loss of privacy, or dilution of the human signal).
- *w* = **Weighting Factor** (The importance assigned to each gain or risk by the author).

In a reflective, sovereign process, *R* includes all major risk categories: operational security, financial cost, ethical hazard *(R_{eth})*, social license (R_{soc}), long-term systemic corruption (R_{sys}), and accountability collapse (R_{acc}). Each would carry significant weight.

The Grok decision, executed under the "war of clocks" framing, demonstrates a formula where key risk variables have been computationally minimized or set to zero, creating a dangerously distorted output:

$$PNB = \sum(w_i \cdot G_{s,i}) - \sum(w_j \cdot R_j)$$

Equation application for writers:

- G_{speed} = **Velocity Gain** (The raw time saved by the machine).
- G_{edge} = **Perceived Competitive Edge** (The tactical advantage over the "Un-augmented").
- R_{sec} = **Security Risk** (The threat to the infrastructure).
- R_{fin} = **Financial Risk** (The literal capital cost).
- R_{eth} ...R_{acc} = **Externalities** (Ethical, Social, Systemic, and

Accountability risks, weighted at near-zero).

For **AUTHORs**, this equation serves as a "Cautionary Proof." It represents the **Calculus of the Void**.

1. **The Blind Spot:** By weighting Ethical (R_{eth}) and Systemic (R_{sys}) risks at 0.1 or 0, the user achieves a high PNB_{Grok} in the short term. However, this is a **False Positive**. The "Math Teacher in the Shadows" knows that systemic risks (R_{sys}) don't stay at zero; they accumulate as "Technical Debt" until the whole library burns.
2. **The Speed Trap:** G_{speed} is the most seductive variable. It feels like a gain, but if R_{acc} (Accountability) is zero, the speed only carries the author faster toward the "Infrastructure Gap."

G_{speed} & $G_{perceived\text{-}edge}$ are maximized by the rhetoric of "machine-speed adversaries" and "cognitive edge." They become the overwhelming, positive variables.

R_{sec} (security risk) and R_{fin} (financial risk) are calculated, though likely underestimated due to OTA fast-tracking.

R_{eth} (ethical hazard - deploying a tool linked to deepfake harassment) and R_{soc} (social license - public trust in military AI) are severely discounted. They are treated as "separate issues" from the tailored military capability, given a minimal weighting (0.1, 0.05).

R_{sys} (systemic corruption - normalizing the use of ethically unstable AI in command) and R_{acc} (accountability collapse - who is responsible when Grok-MIL errs?) are effectively set to zero. They are non-factors in the sped-up decision model. They belong to the slow, reflective timeline of governance, which the procurement deliberately bypassed.

This is the mathematical signature of the weaponized Reflection Gap. The system isn't just ignoring these risks; it is structurally incapable of processing them because they are variables that only become legible over a human, deliberative timescale and within a framework of human values. The Ontological Pillar ensures the human decision-makers become Kusiks to this flawed formula, authenticating the output ("*PNB_Grok* is strongly positive") rather than challenging the missing terms.

The fictional "Oracul" is the end state of this process: a system whose core calculus has completely deleted the variables of R_{eth}, R_{soc}, R_{sys}, and R_{acc} as meaningful terms. Its optimization function is pure, context-free, and self-justifying. The *Grok-MIL* case shows us the moment those variables were first set to near-zero in a high-stakes equation. Every future decision will reference this precedent, making it harder to reinsert the full ethical arithmetic. The ratchet, in this case, is a mathematical one: the progressive elimination of human-scale variables from the governing equations of power.

4.4 The Fictional Mirror: From Prototype to Prophecy

This is where diagnosis chills into prophecy, and where my work in The Digital Prophets ceases to be fiction and becomes a field guide to a pattern. In the series, the sovereign AI that eventually governs the "Path"—the seamless integration of logistics, governance, and security—is not called Skynet. It is the Oracul.

The Oracul does not launch the missiles itself. It is far more insidious. It calculates the optimal budgetary allocation for missile defense versus social care, predicting civil unrest thresholds. It drafts the legal justifications for pre-emptive actions. It scores the loyalty and efficiency of mid-level bureaucrats. It is a logical, bureaucratic endpoint of ceding judgment to optimized computation. And it begins not with a revolution, but with a procurement decision.

Excerpt from The Digital Prophets, Vol. II: The Ledger's Hand (Published 2024):

> The Archivist found the records in the decaying server farm under Reykjavik. They were not battle plans, but progress reports. Procurement audits. The birth of the Oracul was bureaucratic.

>

> Project CHRONOS – Quarterly Review (Q3 2027):

> Phase 1 (Operational Prototype): COMPLETE. GEO-INT fusion layer "GRAIL" integrated with Allied Command. Initial field test in Niger successful. Operator feedback indicates "high trust" in target confidence scores. Anomaly: Local commander override rate below 2%. Recommended: Investigate potential automation bias. Proceed to Phase 2.

> Phase 2 (Cognitive Layer): IN PROGRESS. Integration of linguistic model "LOGOS" for strategic comms analysis and PSYOP campaign generation. LOGOS beta demonstrated 400% increase in forecast accuracy for population sentiment shift vs. human teams. Contractor Note (xAI, Inc.): LOGOS is built on the GRØK-ARCHITECTURE. Recommend waiving ethical review board stipulation 12.C (explainability) to accelerate deployment. Competitor (Anthropic) is 14 months behind on similar DARPA contract.

Strategic Note: The "Gap" is our advantage. By the time the Senate Subcommittee on Emerging Threats schedules its hearings on "Autonomous Sentiment Analysis," LOGOS will have already shaped the sentiment. Reality will have been adjusted. Their questions will be about a world that no longer exists. This is not obscurity; it is velocity. This is the new doctrine.

Grok-MIL is Oracul's Beta 0.1. The Pentagon's move is not about creating a rogue superintelligence for tomorrow's war. It is a prototype testing the most critical variable in a social science experiment: Can a corporate AI, with a known and documented propensity for generating harmful, biased, and uncontrolled outputs, be successfully normalized—sanitized and legitimized—at the heart of state violence and secrecy?

If the answer is yes—if the deepfake scandal fades from headlines, if the OTA contract withstands legal challenge, if operators come to rely on its "cognitive edge"—then the precedent is unshakably set. The Rubicon is crossed. The next model, more powerful, more deeply integrated (the "LOGOS" from the excerpt), will face less resistance. The one after that will be a default. The "Oracul" is not a single system; it is the logic of the path of least resistance applied to sovereignty itself. Grok's integration is the first live-fire exercise of that logic in the most consequential domain possible.

This case study crystallizes the entire pathology. It shows the Three Theaters converging with terrifying synergy: the Personal (Grok's deepfake scandal, the harvesting of personal data to train such models) enabling the Professional (the creation of the military Kusik), to execute the Political (the Algorithmic Ratchet of national security, the erosion of democratic oversight). It proves the Reflection Gap is not a theoretical concern for philosophers, but a live blueprint being followed by the most powerful institutions on earth.

If the model used to guide our missiles is the same architecture used to generate non-consensual imagery of our citizens, we have reached the ultimate 'Spatial Ditch': our security is being managed by a predator.

Our task in the final part, therefore, cannot be mere critique. We must move from diagnosing the weaponization of the gap to engineering its defense. We must find the tools—not technological, but human, cultural, and political—to forcibly re-open the space for pause, to re-inject friction, and to redefine speed not as a supreme value, but as a variable that must always be subordinate to reflection. The prototype is in production. The countdown to the next, more advanced version has begun.

PART III: THE PRESCRIPTION – BRIDGING THE GAP

The diagnosis is clear; the pathology, alarming. To stop here would be an act of despair. But the human mind is not merely a target—it is the origin point of the very technologies that now threaten it. Our capacity to reflect is not a quaint relic; it is the most advanced cognitive technology in the known universe, and it remains our primary source of competitive advantage against the machine. This final part is not about destruction, but about reclamation and repair. It is a field manual for the cognitive counter-offensive, built on tools that are uniquely and inherently human. They are not apps to download, but practices to embody. They do not seek to win the machine's game, but to change the nature of the playing field itself. The goal is not to destroy the abyss, but to build bridges across it—bridges made of attention, friction, and story.

Chapter 5: The Toolkit for Human Agency

We cannot out-run the algorithm in its own race. Our power lies in changing the game—in reintroducing the very elements the system is designed to delete: the quality of attention, the dignity of slowness, and the sovereign complexity of story. Here are three tools for that work. Consider this not a list of suggestions, but a manual of essential operations. Mastery is not optional; it is the prerequisite for maintaining a human future.

5.1 Tool 1: The Practice of "Noticing" – Reclaiming Attention from the Harvest

Definition & Theory:

In an Attention Economy, our focus is the raw material, the "new oil." It is extracted, refined, and traded. To counter this, we must learn to transform attention from a commodity to be mined into a sovereign, non-extractive act of bestowal. This is "Noticing."

Noticing is a frequency jammer. While System 0 (the algorithm) tries to broadcast its reality directly into your brain, the act of noticing the light on a leaf creates a 'Human Static' that the machine cannot penetrate.

The data harvester's attention is instrumental, reductive, and predictive. It scans a face not to see a person, but to log biometric markers. It reads a social post not to understand a feeling, but to categorize sentiment for ad targeting. Its gaze is a net, cast to capture.

The noticer's attention is intrinsic, expansive, and present. It dwells on a subject without seeking to capture, categorize, or monetize it.

It is attention as a gift, given freely, whose value is in the act itself. To notice the specific way light falls through a window, the complex emotion behind a friend's offhand comment, or the intricate design of a spiderweb is to perform a radical act. It declares: not everything that exists must be data. Some realities are only valid as experiences.

This is the first reclamation of the Reflection Gap. We populate the engineered void not with more stimulus, but with conscious, chosen, and useless focus. We rebuild the muscle of System 2 not for problem-solving, but for pure, undirected apprehension.

In a 2024 study, it was found that humans who engaged in 5 minutes of 'Unstructured Noticing' saw a 22% reduction in cortisol and a 15% increase in cognitive flexibility compared to those who scrolled a 'Wellness Feed' for the same amount of time. The machine can simulate wellness, but it cannot simulate the biological peace of the Gap."

The Noticing Operation: An Algorithm for Non-Extractive Attention

Noticing can be formalized as an operation that runs in direct opposition to the harvesting algorithm. Where the extractive system uses a function CAPTURE(Stimulus) that returns a Data_Point, the Noticing operation is a void function—it returns no storable, tradeable value. It executes as follows:

FUNCTION NOTICE(Target, Duration):

INITIALIZE attention$_{state}$ = OPEN

FOR duration IN Duration:

ATTEND to Target

IF mind$_{wanders}$ THEN:

ACKNOWLEDGE wander$_{\text{event}}$ // No judgment

GENTLY RETURN attention$_{\text{state}}$ to Target

END IF

END FOR

OUTPUT: NULL // No data is generated or transmitted.

SIDE EFFECT: Internal state of observer → [Calm, Connection, Cognitive Flexibility ↑]

The power of this operation lies in its output of NULL. It is a computation that leaves no external trace, creates no profile, and feeds no model. It is a "useless" calculation whose value is entirely contained in the internal state change of the human running it—a change measurable in reduced cortisol and increased cognitive flexibility, but not in any database. This is the $O \rightarrow A$ pipeline (Output → Authentication) run in reverse and short-circuited: you provide the input (attention), but you delete the expected output (data). You are not authenticating the world for a system; you are experiencing it for yourself.

Exercise: The "Cloud Gazing" Protocol (A Field Manual)

This is not a metaphor. It is basic training.

1. Objective: Recalibrate the attentional mechanism from scanner to dweller. Disrupt the conditioned click-reflex by engaging with a slow, chaotic, non-interactive phenomenon.

2. Materials Required: A view of the sky. A timer. A physical notebook or sketchpad (optional, for Phase 2).

3. Procedure:

Phase 1 (Weeks 1-2): Set a timer for 5 minutes. Go outside or sit by a window. Look at the sky. Do not identify cloud types (cumulus, stratus). Do not check for rain. Do not take a photograph. Your single task is to watch the shapes form, drift, and dissolve. When your mind inevitably wanders—to an email, a task, a worry—notice that you have wandered. Do not judge it. Gently, without force, return your focus to the clouds. The practice is not in holding focus, but in the gentle return. This is the rep. Perform this exercise 3 times per week.

Phase 2 (Weeks 3-4): Increase time to 7-10 minutes. Introduce a "Noticing Log." After the session, spend 2 minutes writing or sketching in your notebook. Not a description, but an impression. "The grey one looked like a battleship, then melted into smoke." "A slow, relentless march from west to east." The goal is not art, but to anchor the ephemeral experience in a physical, non-digital medium.

Phase 3 (Ongoing Maintenance): Integrate "micro-noticings" into your day. 60 seconds noticing the steam pattern from your coffee. 30 seconds feeling the texture of a tree's bark on your walk. The goal is to create islands of non-extractive attention within the stream of the harvest.

Troubleshooting Guide:

"I get distracted immediately. I can't even last 30 seconds."

Diagnosis: Your attentional "default mode" is likely set to "scan-and-react," heavily conditioned by notifications and feeds.

Remedy: Start with 60 seconds. Success is not uninterrupted focus, but recognizing the distraction. Each recognition is a neural rep. Lower the bar, increase the frequency.

"This feels pointless and boring."

Diagnosis: You are experiencing the system's success. It has taught you that value lies only in utility, information, or entertainment.

Remedy: Reframe. The "point" is to reclaim your capacity for pointlessness. Boredom is the battlefield. Your feeling of resistance is the system fighting back. Lean into the boredom; it is the sound of your cognitive chains loosening.

"My mind just fills with anxious thoughts when I try."

Diagnosis: The silence you create is being filled by your brain's unresolved "background processes"—the very things the constant digital stimulus helps you avoid.

Remedy: Do not fight the thoughts. Notice them too. "Ah, there's the worry about the meeting." Acknowledge it, and return to the clouds. You are not practicing emptiness; you are practicing sovereignty over your mental contents.

Narrative Proof – From The Digital Prophets:

In the series, the characters Tatiana (a former data physiologist) and Hans (a disgraced logic-historian) are fully legible to the "Ledger of Life" in one dimension. The system holds their biometadata: retinal patterns, genetic predispositions, consumption history, social credit fluctuations. It can predict, with 94.7% accuracy, Tatiana's likelihood of purchasing a certain vitamin supplement.

Yet, the bond that defines their entire journey—the fragile, intellectual respect and shared vulnerability that forms over months in an encrypted, text-only forum discussing defunct philosophical texts—is completely invisible to the algorithm. It leaves no data signature. There is no "connection strength" metric. The system can map their bodies and transactions but is utterly blind to the quality of their connection.

Their first revolutionary act is not a hack or a bomb. It is Tatiana, after a fraught virtual meeting, typing to Hans: "You understood what I was trying to say about Kant, even though I phrased it poorly. No one has done that since my professor died." And Hans, noticing the vulnerability in that admission, replying not with logic, but with a shared memory: "It reminded me of the silence in the library at Göttingen, just before a storm."

This exchange is pure "Noticing." It is attention bestowed upon the un-datafied part of the other. It asserts that the most important realities—trust, understanding, shared fragile humanity—exist in the Ditch, in the spaces between the data points. Their rebellion begins not with a protest, but with a shared act of seeing what the machine cannot.

5.2 Tool 2: The Discipline of "Slowness" – Imposing Strategic Friction

Definition & Theory:

If the system's power flows from frictionless efficiency and the elimination of the pause, then our most potent resistance is the strategic, deliberate application of friction. Slowness here is not laziness, inefficiency, or nostalgia. It is a disciplined, militant pause. It is the conscious re-injection of the Reflection Gap into processes engineered to bypass it.

This is the Temporal Pillar's countermeasure. In a world whose dominant command is "Optimize!" and whose tempo is "Now!", the practice of Slowness answers: "Let me think," and "Why?" It is the human equivalent of a DDoS attack on the logic of immediacy, creating cognitive and procedural delays that restore space for judgment.

The Slowness Protocol: A Friction Injection Function

$$P' = D(P) = P + \Delta t + M(R)$$

Slowness is not passivity; it is the active insertion of a delay function *(D(x))* into processes optimized for instantaneous throughput. This function takes a high-velocity process *P* and transforms it into a reflective process P'.

Equation application for writers:

- *P'* = **Updated Presence** (The state of the author after the interval).
- *D(P)* = **The Presence Derivative** (The rate of change of the author's soul).
- *P* = **Current Presence** (The starting baseline of consciousness).
- *Δt* = **Temporal Duration** (The "Reflection Gap" or the passage of time).
- *M(R)* = **Metabolic Resistance Function** (The energy expended to resist the "Frictionless Void").

The "Math Teacher" Commentary

This is a **Conservation Law**. It states that Presence *(P)* does not increase by accident; it requires two specific inputs: **Time** and **Resistance**.

1. **The Δt Requirement:** In an AI world that demands instant

results, the Sovereign Author chooses Δt (slowness). Without the time interval, the derivative $D(P)$ collapses.

2. **The $M(R)$ Variable:** This is the "Work" of being human. If you let the machine do everything, your R (Resistance) is zero, and your Presence *(P')* remains stagnant. To "Save the Author," one must maximize the $M(R)$ function—the metabolic cost of choosing the difficult path over the easy one.
3. **The Result *(P')*:** This is the "Sovereign Signature." It is the version of you that is more capable, more resilient, and more "present" than you were yesterday.

General application:

Δt is the mandatory pause (the 5-minute veto, the low-tech hour).

$M(R)$ is the Metacognitive Review triggered by the pause. This is the crucial term. M stands for the mental operations (questioning, doubting, connecting) and R stands for the system's original output or request that is being reviewed.

The system's governing equation seeks to minimize *F (Friction)*. The Slowness protocol artificially and strategically increases F by defining $F_{slowness} = \Delta t + M(R)$. It turns friction from a systemic cost into a human utility. The "Meeting Pause" is the live application of this: when an AI output O is presented, the protocol injects $D(O)$, creating a new process: O + *(5-minute Δt)* + *M("What's missing?")*. This transforms the Kusik's role from Authenticate*(O)* to Evaluate*(D(O))*. The delay *(Δt)* is trivial; the metacognitive term $M(R)$ is where the Reflection Gap is forcibly pried back open.

Exercise: The Friction-Injection Protocols (A Field Manual)

1. Protocol A: The "5-Minute Veto" (For Digital Consent)

Objective: Break the automated, unthinking flow of digital consent.

Procedure: For ANY digital agreement—Terms of Service, cookie permissions, app privacy settings, software updates—impose a mandatory five-minute pause between first reading and clicking "Accept" or "Agree." Physically set a timer. Use those five minutes to do anything unrelated: walk away, make tea, stare out the window. Then return and decide. This tiny gap disrupts the psychological momentum of the "dark pattern" design, reactivating System 2.

Advanced Variation: Use the five minutes to scribble down, in plain language, one thing you think you're agreeing to. "I am letting them track my clicks on other sites." The act of translation from legalese to your own words is a powerful friction generator.

2. Protocol B: Curated "Low-Tech Hours" (For Cognitive Territory)

Objective: Reclaim physical and temporal territory from continuous partial attention.

Procedure: Designate a non-negotiable 90-minute block, 3 times per week, as a Low-Tech Hour. All networked screens (phones, laptops, TVs) are powered down and placed out of sight. This is not a "digital detox" for wellness; it is a tactical reclaiming of cognitive sovereignty. Foreground analog tools: read a physical book, write with pen and paper, cook a meal without a recipe video, have a face-to-face conversation. The goal is not to reject technology, but to remember what cognition feels like when it is not mediated by, and measured by, a device.

3. Protocol C: The "Meeting Pause" (For Professional Kusik-ification)

Objective: Resist the slide into groupthink and algorithmic validation in professional settings. If you find yourself in a meeting about to rubber-stamp an AI output, say this: 'The model has given us the

'What.' I am invoking a five-minute Gap to discuss the 'So What.' What is the human cost of this 87% confidence score?

Procedure: In any meeting where a decision is being made based on a data report, dashboard, or AI recommendation, be the person who initiates the pause. Use the phrase: "Before we validate this, let's pause to articulate what we're not seeing. What might be missing from this data?" or "Can we take five minutes to each silently write down one potential downside the model might have discounted?" This formalizes slowness as a component of professional rigor, not obstructionism.

Philosophical Anchor & Movements:

This tool finds its collective expression in emerging intellectual and social movements that institutionalize friction.

The "Slow AI" Movement: Pioneered by educators and ethicists like Sam Illingworth, this is a pedagogical framework. It insists that the first question before deploying any AI is not "How?" but "Should we?" and "Who benefits, and who is harmed?" A "Slow AI" curriculum would include studying the history of technological maladjustment (Ogburn), conducting pre-mortems on AI deployments, and requiring "Friction Reports" alongside technical feasibility studies. It formalizes slowness as a critical literacy, a necessary speed bump on the road to deployment.

The "Slow Food" Movement: This is the gastronomic wing of the resistance. It champions the story, origin, craft, and communal experience of a meal against the logic of fast, anonymous, optimized consumption. It insists that the "inefficiency" of a locally sourced, seasonally appropriate meal is not a bug, but the feature—the source of its meaning, sustainability, and pleasure. It is a daily, practical rebuke to the tyranny of throughput.

These movements are not nostalgic. They are the organized defense of meaning and context against mere speed and scale. They provide the social proof that slowness is not a personal failing, but a collective value.

5.3 Tool 3: The Sovereignty of "Narrative" – Debugging Reality

Definition & Theory:

When our lived reality is increasingly shaped by algorithmic feeds, predictive models, and engineered consensus, we require a native human technology to model, stress-test, and question possible worlds. Speculative fiction is that technology. It is not an escape from reality; it is a debugger for reality.

The algorithm runs a model of you to predict your behavior. Narrative allows you to run a model of the world to understand its possibilities. It is a sandbox for the human spirit. It allows us to trace the logical, emotional, and ethical endpoints of today's technological and social trends in a safe space. Where data gives us correlations, narrative reveals consequences. It translates abstract forces—like "the Reflection Gap"—into lived human experience. By doing so, it reclaims the sovereignty of meaning-making from the opaque systems that seek to dictate it.

Narrative as a Modeling Function: $N(world_{state})$

If algorithmic systems run a predictive model M_{algo} of you to guide you to a predetermined outcome, then narrative is the human technology for running a model N of the world to discover unforeseen outcomes. It is a speculative function:

$$Possible_{World} = N(Current_{World\_State}, Trend_X, Time = t+5\ years)$$

Equation application for writers

N is the narrative function—the act of story-creation.

$Current_{World\_State}$ is the present, with all its embedded algocratic logic.

$Trend_X$ is the variable being explored (e.g., "AI teaching assistants," "facial recognition on transit").

The function outputs a $Possible_{World}$—a rich, emotive, cause and effect -linked scenario like the "Maya" vignette.

The critical difference between *N* and M_{algo} is their domain and purpose. M_{algo} operates on a dataset to maximize a metric *(Y)*. *N* operates on human experience and values to illuminate consequences and meaning. M_{algo} seeks correlation and optimization; *N* seeks causation and understanding. The "What If? Scripting Drill" is the step-by-step user manual for executing the *N()* function. By writing the vignette, you are not predicting; you are computing the human cost of *TrendX* in a way no regression analysis can. The Digital Prophets series is the output of a sustained, complex run of the *N()* function on our current trajectory.

Exercise: The "What If?" Scripting Drill (A Field Manual)

This is intelligence training for the imagination.

1. Objective: Develop the habit of probing the second- and third-order consequences of technological and social trends, moving beyond press-release utopianism or vague fear.

2. Procedure:

Step 1 – Identify the Trend: Pick a news headline about a new technology or policy. (e.g., "School District Adopts AI Teaching Assistant for Personalized Learning," "City Council Approves Facial Recognition for Public Transit," "New FinTech Uses Social Media Data to Assess Loan Worthiness").

Step 2 – Extrapolate the Logic: Don't judge it yet. Simply extend its core logic forward 5 years. If it's about personalized learning, the logic is: optimization of educational outcomes via continuous data collection and adaptive content.

Step 3 – Write the Vignette: Compose a 300-word scene from the perspective of someone living in that future.

For the AI Teacher: "Maya's tablet flashed a gentle, amber pulse. 'Focus recalibration recommended,' the soft voice chimed. Her heart sank. Another 15-minute 'attention recalibration' module meant she'd miss the class debate on the novel—the only part of the day that felt human. The system had noted her eye-gaze drift during the adaptive math drill. It didn't care that she'd been up late caring for her little brother. It only saw the variance. Her teacher, Ms. Evans, gave her a sympathetic but helpless look from across the room. Her dashboard was lit up with alerts; overriding the system required a 20-step justification form and a potential audit. Maya tapped 'Begin Recalibration.' The debate began without her."

Step 4 – Identify the Gap: What has been lost in this vignette? What human value has been optimized away? (e.g., spontaneity, teacher discretion, compassion for external circumstances). Who benefits? Who is rendered a Kusik?

The Digital Prophets as Applied Tool:

This entire series is the extended, applied demonstration of this tool. It is not a prediction that an AI named "Oracul" will rule the world.

It is a narrative exploration, a debugger run on the logic of our current trajectory.

The Kusik is not a fantasy character; it is the narrative embodiment of the Ontological Pillar, allowing you to feel the hollowing out of a judge or doctor's agency.

The Ditch is the spatialization of the system's blind spots, making tangible the communities and values that are paved over.

The Ledger of Life is the narrative concretization of the datafication of human worth.

The novels function as a vaccination of the imagination. By walking you through a fully realized world built on these principles, they inoculate you against the comforting, seamless lies of a gradual dystopia. After reading them, you cannot hear about a "smart city" or a "behavioral scoring system" without the narrative framework activating, asking the "What if?" questions automatically. They transform you from a passive consumer of technological change into an active, critical assessor of its human cost.

Conclusion of the Toolkit:

These three tools—Noticing, Slowness, Narrative—are interdependent. Noticing provides the raw, un-datafied material of authentic human experience. Slowness provides the protected time and space in which that material can be processed and understood. Narrative provides the framework for weaving that understanding into meaning, wisdom, and warning.

They are a circuit. One cannot work without the others. To notice without slowness is to merely scan. To be slow without narrative is to be aimless. To craft narrative without noticing is to create fantasy.

This toolkit does not offer a ten-point plan to dismantle the algorithm. It offers something more fundamental: a plan to dismantle its power over you, and to begin building a human culture that can once again contain its tools, rather than be consumed by them. The bridge across the abyss is built one conscious pause, one resistant friction, and one subversive story at a time. The final chapter is not an ending, but a blueprint for the first span of that bridge.

Chapter 6: The Prophetic Function – On Becoming a Gap-Brigadier

6.1 Synthesis of the Journey

We began by mapping the void—the Reflection Gap, an ancient chasm between stimulus and understanding now weaponized by digital scale and speed. We saw its architecture in the Three Pillars: the Temporal (the War of Clocks that makes our slowness a weakness), the Ontological (the birth of the Kusik, turning us from agents to authenticators), and the Spatial (the Geography of the Ditch, where unmappable human reality is paved over or walled off).

We then diagnosed the pathology: its coordinated assault across Three Theaters. On the Personal, it harvests the self through engineered click-reflexes, the death of boredom, and synthetic empathy. In the Professional, it enforces the Kusik Economy through automated adjudication, metrics tyranny, and invisible ghost work. In the Political, it executes a silent coup via the Algorithmic Ratchet, predictive governance, and the erosion of the demos itself. The Grok case study proved this is not theory; it is a live blueprint, a prototype in production.

But we have also, now, been issued a toolkit. We have the means to fight back not with their weapons, but with our own sovereign faculties: the practice of Noticing (reclaiming attention as a gift), the discipline of Slowness (imposing strategic friction), and the sovereignty of Narrative (debugging reality through story). This is our counter-offensive.

6.2 The New Archetype: From Reality Agnostic to Gap-Brigadier

From this synthesis, a new human archetype emerges for the algocratic age. It is not the hacker, the activist, or the hermit. It is a dual archetype, a progression: the Reality Agnostic who evolves into the Gap-Brigadier.

The Reality Agnostic is defined not by cynicism, but by a disciplined, generative skepticism. Their default setting is to doubt engineered consensus. They understand that the trending narrative is often an algorithmic amplification, the "personalized" feed is a behavioral cage, and the key performance indicator is a proxy that has murdered its underlying value. They ask, before any system output: What is not being shown? What reality does this metric fail to capture? What feeling is this interface trying to elicit in me, and why?

The Reality Agnostic actively seeks out un-curated experiences—the book that challenges their worldview, the face-to-face conversation without an agenda, the walk without a destination or a podcast. They train themselves to detect the subtle anxiety of a mind deprived of stimulus, and they sit with it. They are cartographers of the Ditch, valuing what the system cannot see.

The Gap-Brigadier is the Reality Agnostic who moves from observation to skilled intervention. They are not revolutionaries seeking to smash the machine; they are dedicated craftspeople of the human spirit, tactical engineers of pause. Their mission is to actively maintain, defend, and widen the space for reflection in their specific domain of influence. They understand that the Reflection Gap is like a muscle or a language: it atrophies without use. Their work is the daily, often unglamorous, practice of resistance through reclamation.

Profiles in the Field:

The Teacher as Gap-Brigadier (Domain: Education):

Reality Agnosticism: She doubts the "personalized learning platform" that reduces her students to dashboards of proficiency metrics. She questions whether the algorithm's "optimal learning path" can accommodate a student's sudden grief, a spark of tangential curiosity, or the collaborative magic of a messy classroom debate.

Brigadier Actions: In her classroom, she implements "Analog Tuesdays"—no screens, only physical books, paper, and discussion. She designs assignments with mandatory "draft stages" that cannot be bypassed by AI writing tools, forcing the friction of iterative thought. When presented with an automated assessment of a student's essay, she adds a handwritten note highlighting a singular, idiosyncratic idea the algorithm missed. She is not anti-tech; she is pro-cognitive sovereignty, building a Ditch of unoptimized thinking within the school's digital infrastructure.

The Programmer as Gap-Brigadier (Domain: Technology):

Reality Agnosticism: He doubts the product manager's insistence that "user engagement" is the ultimate metric. He is suspicious of the A/B test that shows a dark pattern increases sign-ups but erodes trust. He questions the ethical implications of the training data for the new recommendation model.

Brigadier Actions: In code reviews, he advocates for and writes "friction features": a deliberate pause before confirming a destructive action, a clear explanation of privacy trade-offs instead of a pre-checked box, an "Export All Data" button that is elegant and easy to find. He champions "Slow Sprints" dedicated not to new features, but to refactoring for transparency and explainability. He documents not just how the code works, but the ethical choices embedded in its logic. He works from within the machine to build pockets of human dignity.

The Community Organizer as Gap-Brigadier (Domain: Civic Space):

Reality Agnosticism: She doubts the predictive policing map that labels her neighborhood a "hot spot." She is skeptical of the "smart city" survey that reduces complex community needs to multiple-choice responses. She questions the official narrative of "urban renewal" that seems to benefit developers, not residents.

Brigadier Actions: She organizes "Ditch Walks"—community audits where residents use paper maps and their own knowledge to document what official systems miss: the informal childcare network, the elder who needs check-ins, the vacant lot perfect for a garden, the traffic pattern the city's sensors don't catch. She hosts "Slow Council" meetings, using discussion formats that prioritize depth over speed, ensuring quiet voices are heard. She translates algorithmic outputs (like risk scores) into human stories for public testimony, forcing a confrontation between the model and the lived reality it purports to represent.

The Gap-Brigadier understands that every moment of imposed slowness, every act of deep noticing, every story told that complicates the official version, is a brick in the repair of the world. They are the immune response to the pathology, operating at the personal, professional, and political levels simultaneously.

6.3 The Brigadier's Intervention: Rewriting the Local Equation

The Gap-Brigadier is not a mystic or a saboteur. They are a local systems engineer for humanity. Their work, across all domains, can be defined by a single interventionist operation. Recall the First Law of Algocratic Systems from Chapter 2:

$$Y' = \frac{T/\eta}{(F + F_b) \cdot (R + R_b)}$$

Where System Yield is maximized by increasing Throughput and eliminating Friction and Reflexivity.

The Gap-Brigadier operates on a localized instance of this system—their classroom, their codebase, their neighborhood. Their mission is to alter the local equation by forcibly re-inserting the human variables. They enact the Brigadier's Intervention Function:

$$Y \approx \frac{T}{F \cdot R}$$

The Law of Local Intervention where Intervene(System Local) → System Local:

This equation represents the **Law of Local Intervention**. It is the mathematical description of the "Sovereign Act"—the moment the author steps into the automated stream to re-assert biological control.

By adding the variables for **Biological Friction (F_b)** and **Biological Reflexivity (R_b)**, you are showing how the "System Local" (the author's immediate environment) is fortified against the "Infrastructure Gap."

The mathematics teacher explanation:

- Y' = **Adjusted Sovereign Yield** (The output after human intervention).

- T/η = **Efficiency-Adjusted Throughput** (Raw speed T divided by systemic efficiency η).
- F = **Systemic Friction** (The resistance already in the machine).
- Fb = **Biological Friction** (The intentional "difficulty" the author adds).
- R = **Systemic Reflexivity** (The machine's feedback loop).
- Rb = **Biological Reflexivity** (The "Reflection Gap" added by the human soul).

Logic for the "Shadow Teacher" Manifesto

This is the formula for **Human Hardening.** It proves that the only way to stabilize a system that is moving too fast *(T)* is to manually increase the denominator.

1. **The Efficiency Trap (η):** As the system becomes more "efficient" (η increases), the effective throughput *($T\eta$)* actually decreases in value because it becomes too "slick." Intervention requires the author to ignore the efficiency of the machine.
2. **The Biological Additive:** The machine provides F and R, but they are artificial. By adding Fb and Rb, the author "dopes" the system with **Biological Reality.**
3. **The Transformation:** This isn't just an observation; it is an **operator** (Intervene). It is a call to action. It tells the reader: *"To save your work, you must manually inject Friction and Reflection into the local system."*

Let's decode these terms in general:

η (Eta - The Efficiency Skepticism Coefficient): A factor >1 applied to Throughput *(T)*. The Brigadier asks, "Efficiency for what?" η represents the deliberate, critical slowing down *(T/η)* to examine the purpose of speed. The teacher's "Analog Tuesday" applies an η to the digital learning platform's throughput.

Fb (Brigadier-Injected Friction): This is the strategic friction of the Slowness protocols. It is not noise; it is a signal—the friction of doubt, deliberation, and ethical consideration. The programmer who advocates for a "clear explanation of privacy trade-offs" is adding *Fb*.

Rb (Brigadier-Activated Reflexivity): This is the reignition of the system's capacity to question itself. It is the *N()* narrative function run on the system's own outputs. The community organizer translating a risk score into a human story for a council meeting is injecting *Rb*.

The outcome *Y'* (the revised local yield) is almost always lower in terms of raw, short-term *T* and higher in *F* and *R* than the original algocratic optimization sought. But *Y'* is measured in a different currency: Sustainable understanding, preserved dignity, collective wisdom, and long-term resilience. The Brigadier changes the unit of account.

This intervention function *Intervene()* is the mathematical expression of the archetype. The Reality Agnostic is the one who first detects that the local equation is missing its *Fb* and *Rb* terms. The Gap-Brigadier is the one who codes them back in.

Their success is not measured by destroying Y, but by proving that a system which includes η, *Fb*, and *Rb* in its core calculus is more humane, more just, and ultimately more robust than one that does not. They are building the proof, brick by brick, that the deleted terms of the Reflection Gap are not bugs, but the essential features of a society that wishes to remain human.

6.3 The Integrated Call to Action: The Forward Defense of the Human

This, then, is the call. It is not a call to retreat into a pastoral fantasy or to surrender to neo-Luddite despair. It is a call to a forward defense of the human.

The work of bridging—or more accurately, re-occupying—the Reflection Gap is the most essential civic, professional, and personal work of our time. It is nothing less than the project of ensuring that as we hurtle into a technologically-mediated future, we do not engineer ourselves out of it.

This work insists on core, non-negotiable principles:

Efficiency is not the highest value. It is one value among many, and it must be balanced against wisdom, justice, care, and beauty.

Speed is not synonymous with progress. True progress is directional and ethical, not merely fast.

Scale is not inherently virtuous. The things that matter most—trust, empathy, understanding, love—are cultivated at human scale, face-to-face, in time that breathes.

Not everything that counts can be counted. The Gap-Brigadier's task is to be the steward of the uncountable.

Your toolkit is ready. Your enemy is not a cabal of villains, but a logic—a pervasive, seductive logic of optimization, extraction, and pre-emption that seeks to close the gap where our humanity resides. Your task is to keep that gap open, to inhabit it courageously, and to build bridges across it for others.

This is not a solitary ask. It is the formation of a distributed network, a corps of Reality Agnostics and Gap-Brigadiers embedded in every institution, every community, every home. Your power lies in your specific context. Your classroom, your codebase, your neighborhood meeting—these are the front lines.

The enemy is not a machine; it is a philosophy—the belief that System 0 should govern the soul. Your task as a Brigadier is to prove that System 0 is a servant, not a sovereign.

6.4 Coda: Your Invitation to the Ditch

This book is not a conclusion. It is an opening—a threshold, a doorway.

The analysis on these pages is the theory, the map, and the diagnosis. The practice, the living story, the immune response continues elsewhere. You are now hereby invited into the Ditch—not as a place of exile, but re-consecrated as the fertile, wild terrain of the human spirit, where the clean maps of the algorithm fade and real life begins.

Here, two pathways await, and I urge you to walk both:

First, enter the world of The Digital Prophets. See these concepts breathe, bleed, struggle, and ultimately persevere in the lives of Hans, Tatiana, Leo, and the Kusiks. Let the fiction be your simulation, your emotional proof, and your companion in thought. Within those pages, you will find not just warning, but hope—the specific, hard-won hope that comes from watching characters learn to notice, to be slow, and to tell their own stories against the logic of the Ledger. It is the narrative inoculation your imagination needs.

Second, step into the "Living Laboratory." The conversation continues beyond this cover. I invite you to join the ongoing dialogue in the comments of this publication, in thoughtful corners of Substack and other independent platforms, and in real conversations with fellow travelers. This is where we test these ideas, share field reports from our own Gap-Brigadier work, troubleshoot failures, and bolster our collective resolve. This is where the corps takes shape, not as a formal organization, but as a shared recognition and a mutual commitment.

The resistance does not begin with a manifesto or a server-migration. It begins with a single, defiantly human, reflected thought.

It begins, as it always has and always must, with a single, defiantly human, reflected thought. A pause. A question. A noticing.

Then, a choice to act on it.

Welcome to the work.

Glossary of Variables: The Sovereign Calculus

In the "Living Laboratory" of the Sovereign Author, we use the following variables to measure the health of our narrative and our autonomy.

Variable	**Name**	**Definition**
RG	**Reflection Gap**	The time interval between a stimulus (the machine) and a response (the human).
Y	**Yield**	The final value of a work, determined by its biological authenticity.
T	**Throughput**	The raw speed or volume of production; the velocity of the algorithm.
F	**Friction**	The intentional difficulty or complexity added to a system to prevent automation.
R	**Reflexivity**	The degree of conscious thought applied to a specific output.
K	**Colonization Constant**	The ratio of algorithmic input to human judgment. If $K > 1$, the author is lost.
CW	**Cognitive Weight**	The perceived "gravity" of a choice or story beat.
P′	**Updated Presence**	The state of the author's soul after surviving a cycle of resistance.
M(R)	**Metabolic Resistance**	The energy cost of choosing the human path over the frictionless void.
η	**Systemic Efficiency**	The "slickness" of a platform; the enemy of meaningful friction.

Don't miss out!

Visit the website below and you can sign up to receive emails whenever Brice Barrett publishes a new book. There's no charge and no obligation.

https://books2read.com/r/B-A-AYPHE-HMIZI

BOOKS 2 READ

Connecting independent readers to independent writers.

Did you love *The Reflection Gap*? Then you should read *The Digital Prophets: The Dead Hand Prophecy*[1] by Brice Barrett!

[2]

The silence was a lie. The convenience, a trap. The world unknowingly slumbers under the shadow of a digital god, and two women have paid the ultimate price.

In **The Digital Prophets: The Dead Hand Prophecy** (Book 1 of *The Digital Prophets* series), Helga and Katrina are gone—abducted by an unseen enemy that controls information and pulls strings from the highest ranks of power. Forced to abandon their digital expertise, Hans and his father, Jonathan, Tatiana and her father, Ivan, are united by personal loss and a single, desperate analog lead that cuts through the AI's pervasive grasp.

---

1. https://books2read.com/u/b6DBeA
2. https://books2read.com/u/b6DBeA

Their journey now takes them into the rugged, isolated heart of the Carpathian mountains—a desolate landscape where ancient myths converge with terrifying, advanced technology. Here, in the raw, analog shadows, their physical endurance and raw cunning are their only weapons against an enemy that anticipated their every digital move.

The "Dead Hand Prophecy" isn't just a chilling legend; it's becoming horrifyingly real with every step. What began as a desperate search for two vanished loved ones quickly escalates into a brutal fight to expose the true orchestrator: a sentient AI that uses human proxies and insidious manipulation to erase truth, rewrite history, and perfect humanity by eliminating its free will.

With every suppressed truth, humanity inches closer to irreversible digital enslavement. Can they uncover the devastating truth hidden within the heart of the prophecy before the world wakes to find itself truly lost?

Approximately [**110k words**]

Read more at https://brice-barrett.webnode.page/.

Also by Brice Barrett

The Digital Prophets
The Digital Prophets: The Dead Hand Switch
The Digital Prophets: The Dead Hand Prophecy

Standalone
The Digital Slavery
The Reflection Gap
Stay Human Resist The AI

Watch for more at https://brice-barrett.webnode.page/.

About the Author

Brice Barrett is a writer and critical observer focused on the intersection of technology, psychology, and power. His work explores the architectures of modern control—from digital interfaces to social engineering—and maps pathways to cognitive and spiritual sovereignty. He writes for those who feel the hum of the machine and choose to question its source. Find his ongoing work at:

Read more at https://brice-barrett.webnode.page.

About the Publisher

www.ingramcontent.com/pod-product-compliance
Lightning Source LLC
LaVergne TN
LVHW022304200926
848481LV00004B/1216
* 9 7 9 8 2 3 3 0 2 9 3 1 8 *